'This book is pure adventure ~~than that: it's thought-provoki~~ ~~spend extended periods of tir~~ ~~and understanding yourself,~~ Geordie translates the intensity of his experiences beautifully. To complete the feat is one thing, to illuminate what it feels like on the road is another: Geordie has managed to do both. I am a fan.'
*Erling Kagge*

'An extraordinarily sensitive tale of the perils and pleasures of a gritty solo journey. By the end the reader feels they have travelled all the way with the author, enduring all the hardships and enjoying all the rewards. This is the essence of a real travel book.'
*Robin Hanbury-Tenison*

'I haven't come across a journey like this before. Choosing the unfamiliar path is risky but with that comes great insights and rewards. A Rolling Stone is a captivating insight into the mind of a solo traveller. A courageous and bold endeavour.'
*Sir Ranulph Fiennes*

'A Dylan inspired title that captures the wanderlust of our generation. Climbing the Seven Summits and even army deployments seem safe and organised compared to the utter freedom and solitude of the open road for Geordie - leadership is no longer structured, it is a coin toss, a chance meeting, a whim - told with self-deprecating humour, yet thoughtful candour, this two-wheeled adventure is a real page-turner.'
*Mark Beaumont*

'Geordie's remarkable story is a stark and inspirational reminder that the true beauty of life, and of our world, is found when you step out of your comfort zone, journey along new paths and challenge yourself in ways you may never have considered possible. This book is gripping, thought provoking and utterly awe-inspiring.'
*Chrissie Wellington OBE, Four time Ironman World Champion*

'I know from experience it takes courage to embark on a great solo journey. I also know it takes resourcefulness, adaptability and resilience to see it through until the end. Geordie's unexpected choices lead to a fascinating adventure. This book is about taking the road less travelled, venturing into the unknown and coping with uncertainty.'
*Alastair Humphreys*

'A truly wonderful modern adventure, a feat of hardy endurance and immersive travel across high Asia.'
*Levison Wood*

'A true pioneer and an inspiration for tenacity and resilience.'
*Bear Grylls*

# A ROLLING STONE

## TAKING THE ROAD LESS TRAVELLED

### GEORDIE STEWART

Published by Rowan Books

Cover design by Simon Avery

Cover photography by Geordie Stewart

*To my family, for trusting and believing.*

*To Louisa, for bringing kindness and joy to everyone you met.*

# FOREWORD

The romantic ideal of swapping the oppression of the rat race for the freedom of life on the open road is something to which many might aspire, but the story Geordie tells of pedalling away from security and comfort into a world of challenge, uncertainty, loneliness and longing is a telling account of earnest reflection rather than a carefree traveller's yarn.

This is a frank and disarmingly honest account of a continent-crossing odyssey on a second-hand bike, following a route that was chosen more for the remote and monotonous isolation that begets deep introspection, rather than the scenic backdrops that might look good on Instagram. As a result, these pages relate an unvarnished journey of self-discovery; a story of the fripperies of modern life being stripped away as the inescapable scale of the ride takes hold.

There is a saying in Buddhist teaching – 'strong back, soft front' – that emphasises the importance of maintaining a stoic forbearance in the face of reality, while remaining vulnerable and open to the encounters and experiences that come our way. From the desolate Kazakh Steppe in midwinter through bustling Sichuan market towns to the crowded, steamy streets of Kuala Lumpur, it is the littlest of things that shine brightest on this bold adventure: the joy of a fresh wet wipe, the sport of a board game with a Kyrgyz truck driver, the shelter of an empty bus stop in a storm, the gift of fresh pizza from a passing motorist, the kindness of Kazakh cafe owners, the pleasure in a steaming plate of *plov*, a sickly sweet *bánh tiêu* or the solace in a hug from a friend. Geordie's story is peppered with the sorts of joyful hellos and poignant goodbyes that are both milestones and signposts in the life of every human being.

If much of this story is a timeless narrative of human journeying, his time in Xinjiang also brings us face to face with an unsettling contemporary reality. And while his tale of seeing in the New Year alone, shivering in a frozen drainage ditch in northwest China, might shatter any lingering illusions of the allure of solo travel in a far-flung land, his description of the 'warped privilege' at passing through this Orwellian dystopia – when his journey to find freedom leads him to a place of harrowing oppression – is a vital education for us all.

I cannot recall a single day of any of my own expeditions that has been 'OK' or 'not too bad', and Geordie's experiences echo mine. This is a story of soaring highs and crushing lows; a tale that will, I hope, encourage others to set out on journeys of their own, not as a decadent escape from a humdrum existence, but as an opportunity to delve deep into themselves. To experience a life stripped bare, and to test themselves, and the bonds of optimism and hope that hold we humans together, to their very limits.

Ben Saunders

# THE ROUTE

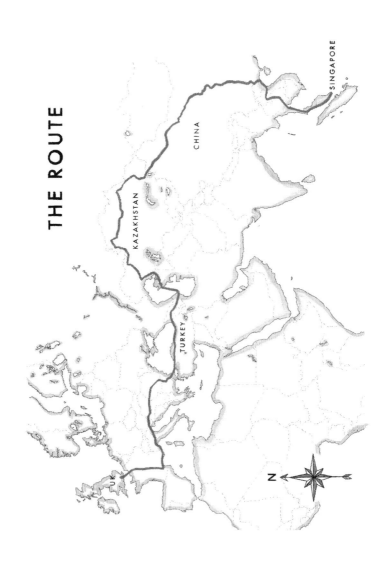

# PROLOGUE

Cycle, eat, sleep, repeat. It was a simple lifestyle in Kazakhstan, the ninth-largest country in the world. The sliver of potholed tarmac snaking its way through the landscape was the only distinguishable feature on the flat, barren, and otherwise featureless horizon. But I was cycling closer to a decision point, a T-junction where I would be forced into conclusive action.

Take a right and there was a road heading southeast towards the Uzbekistan border and the Silk Road: the iconic and accepted route. There was almost a reassuring familiarity in the knowledge of shared suffering and experiences. With winter approaching, it would tick the boxes I wanted: proving to myself my ability to sustain, endure and survive. I might even gain that elusive notion of credibility.

Take a left and I'd commit to the north on a road that wound its way illogically around the edges of the country: close to the Russian border, across the exposed Kazakh Steppe, into Siberia, then the contentious Xinjiang region of northwest China and across the Gobi desert. The very idea of Siberia in mid-winter seemed an absurdity as I rode wearing a T-shirt, shorts and sandals. Nobody I knew had cycled that way. Every logical argument pointed me to the Silk Road.

It is often said a coin toss is the easiest way to make a decision. Quite simply, heads and I turn right, tails and I turn left. People usually regard the essential moment of a coin toss as when and how the coin lands, or perhaps the reveal, when the hand is removed and the decision-making process is out of your control. The key moment is neither. When your heart flutters and your mind hums, the coin is in mid-air and for a split second you know exactly which way you hope it lands. You're willing it to make the decision you internally crave but are yet to openly admit.

I weighed up both options, left or right, time and time again as I pedalled. My mind was drifting from the initial plan. There was a thirst to do something different rather than follow the recognised path, a theme from the inception of this great adventure. I made up my mind. I approached the T-junction and took a left.

I had no idea where I would be staying that evening, let alone for the next few months. It was the beginning of uncertainty and I would have to adapt. I was sure of one thing: these unknown lands were about to become my norm. There was no other option.

# PART I

## ESCAPE

*Nothing behind me, everything ahead of me, as is ever so on the road.*

— Jack Kerouac

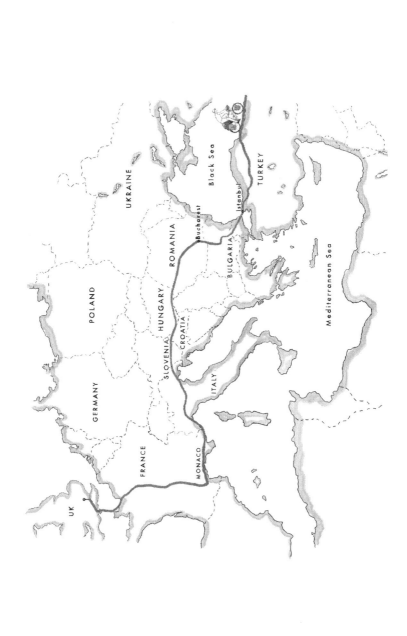

**1.**

After signing off from the army, I had a year-long notice period to find the right job, somewhere I would be a round peg in a round hole. I did personality tests, spoke to and visited friends in different industries: city workers, accountants, lawyers, entrepreneurs, headhunters, sports agents, presenters and writers. Anyone and anything. I wanted to be open-minded, ruling nothing out, in the hope that something might strike a chord. I was seeking that elusive Japanese concept of *ikigai* which roughly translates as 'a reason for being'. It is the combination of mission, vocation, profession and passion. It is the result of finding out what you're good at, what you can be paid for, what the world needs and what you love.

'What would you like to do if money were no object?' The British philosopher Alan Watts posed this simple question in a lecture to his students when asked about vocational guidance. It was a short lecture that I listened to every day as I weighed up options.

Did I want a particular job to facilitate a particular lifestyle or did I want to flee that escalator? Did I want to adhere to what I *should* do, what I was *expected* to do, or choose my own path?

It was not a binary choice. It was not either work hundred-hour weeks in London or become a missionary in a foreign land, but I could not escape the question, 'What would you like to do if money were no object?' I would stretch off after a run and listen to that talk. It was in my headphones as I walked to work. It was often running through my mind as I tried to empty it of all thoughts. It is an idealistic concept because in real life money is, of course, an object, but it made me think.

I have read many accounts of great solo travellers: T. E. Lawrence, Wilfred Thesiger, Paddy Leigh Fermor, Rory Stewart. As the years have progressed, a sense of yearning for my own travels became stronger. Having spent four years climbing the Seven Summits and five years in the British Army, my appetite for travel should have been satiated. Yet, despite those experiences, the idea of solo travel had only started to become more attractive.

My climbing expeditions, long-distance endurance events and military deployments all brought physical and mental hardship. They encouraged teamwork, empathy, leadership and resilience. What they did not provide was the feeling of being isolated. There was usually a support network in place to enable the safety and welfare of the soldiers, climbers or race participants. Measures were put in place to reduce risk and maximise protection.

The journeys that stood out to me were those in which risk, protection, communications and safety were unknowns, where there seemed to be a naïvety and optimism about the traveller who set off unsure of what lay ahead. There appeared an authenticity when the shackles of expectation had been removed and they were forced to adapt to their new environment and lifestyle.

I wanted to go outside my comfort zones and to truly test my character, physically, mentally, emotionally, socially and psychologically. I craved freedom.

If money was no object, if jobs, relationships, expectations and stability were no object, what would I do? The idea came to me gradually but then quickly formed, as though it had always been there, waiting to be plucked from the air. It seemed so simple, so obvious even.

Save money, pack up my life, and leave.

And go where? It could be Alaska, Sydney, Cape Town or Ushuaia. Oddly, the actual destination seemed of little significance.

And how? It had to be by bike. I viewed cycle touring as proper travel. It seemed raw, authentic, difficult and exposed. It was a real way to travel far, meet people and see places. It enabled greater breadth and speed than walking but without the engine, protection and noise of motorbikes or cars. There was something so vulnerable about a solitary cycle tourer and it drew me in. I wanted, I needed, the open road.

My second-hand panniers were filled to the brim; my second-hand bike looked strained under a weight it was unaccustomed to.

Three weeks earlier, I had had no bike, no tent and no panniers. I had been saying for months that I wanted to cycle to the other side of the world, but was so preoccupied with other things, I had barely made inroads into what needed to be done. Those three weeks were a flurry of activity with eBay auctions and Amazon packages arriving in the post. It is easy to overthink big steps into the void. The fear of failure, or fear of the unknown, is often a key factor why people remain where they are.

The Scandinavian concept of the 'doorstep mile' shows that getting started can be the hardest bit; that the first step outside your front door to begin a journey, accepting your new life and leaving behind the old, feels more like a mile. It's the simple reason why so many people don't start.

It is the same reason I was yet to begin a solo journey. It scared me.

I hugely admired my friends who had embarked on big solo trips. I felt my climbing expeditions, although challenging at times, received more credit than they deserved compared to far purer adventures. I read and heard stories about dirty, dusty cyclists somehow surviving in regions where they appeared so out of place. How did they communicate, buy food, sort diplomatic issues and navigate? How did they keep motivated for so long? Where did they sleep? How did they find not being with family and friends for so long?

---

The first drumbeat and guitar strum from 'Like A Rolling Stone' hit my ears. Louder! I turned up the volume again. I have listened to and been captivated by Bob Dylan since I was a teenager. His poetry and prose have resonated with me at different times in my life. No other artist has come close. I've found peace in his melodies, experienced longing from his love songs, wanderlust from his ballads and under-standing from his societal critiques.

I was changing the pedals on my bike but the impact of the song halted my progress and made me stop, sit and think. I had not processed what I was about to undertake. I was so preoccupied packing; I had barely thought about what the journey was going to entail: being truly on my own and being without a home.

The song forced me, albeit briefly, to try to understand what leaving my job, my home, my family and friends would mean. Life on the road, for all the potential highs, would also bring lows I didn't want to imagine. You can read, intellectu-alise and rationalise so much about what might take place, but to understand how it actually feels you need to step into the unknown.

'Okay, Mum, the time has come. I think I'm off now.' I could immediately see tears roll down her cheeks. I couldn't allow myself to do the same; not yet.

She was sitting at the kitchen table at home in Hampshire. So often over the past twenty or so years, I had said something similar. Sometimes for school, other times for expeditions, army deployments, holidays or short bike rides.

'It's odd saying goodbye to someone and not knowing when you'll see them again.' My mum's voice was breaking up as she spoke. Conscious of my own selfishness and guilt, I didn't know how to respond.

I had flippantly told people my journey would take me a couple of years. Part of me wanted to be non-committal, not channelled into having a specific deadline. Part of me didn't want to admit to myself how long this might actually take; I might never have begun. I understood Mum's internal struggle with her son setting off on this journey. Her words, unprepared and maternally instinctive, would remain with me on the thousands of miles ahead.

I gave her a hug and mounted my fully laden bike for the first time. I waved goodbye and then pedalled off. I rounded the corner and put my sunglasses on to hide my tears from the outside world. I didn't look back. I couldn't allow myself to. Only forward from here. A new life.

My timetable was determined by my army leaving date. There was personal and professional satisfaction after my five years but I wanted to begin this trip unemployed and free from my military ID which stated my name, height and rank. Pedalling away through Hampshire towards the coast with a passport and an old Nepalese wallet containing only a pair of bankcards and two €20 notes, I felt completely unfettered.

I was clean-shaven with a grade two haircut; almost a ritual cleansing before the journey could begin. I took the first of hundreds of video diaries I would record over the course of the journey:

> *I've just left home, which is quite scary, quite exciting, quite daunting, quite sad as well. I'm off to Portsmouth, then France and then see where the road takes me, I guess.*

Blissful ignorance, naïvety and enthusiasm. I felt it was important to begin the journey from home. Getting a flight and working back would have been an option but the very idea of choosing to leave seemed significant. Instead of constantly aiming towards home, it was about escaping the very notion of normality. The mindset was different.

About twenty miles outside Portsmouth, the clip on one of my panniers, unaccustomed to the heavy burden now placed upon it, snapped off. I pulled over to the side of the road, removed the panniers and looked around. There was no teammate or friend in sight; nobody with whom to discuss the problem. There was nobody bringing out their repair kit or spare clip to lend to me. It was just me. From now on, it was always going to be just me.

Out came my trusty Leatherman and I managed a workable solution. It was the smallest of lessons I needed. I had chosen to go on this trip alone. I had chosen self-sufficiency over shared experiences. I had chosen independence over teamwork.

The ferry and France followed. It was baguettes, cheese, cured meats, sunflowers and apples pinched from roadside orchards. The August sunshine and consistent schedule of riding and camping made me grateful for the shade and after-noon naps. I was constantly learning: how to find a wild camping spot in a field or a wood, the exact position of kit in my panniers, the best cooking strategies and where to find water filling stations.

Already I was distracted by checkpoints such as crossing a particular river, place names that let my imagination roam and music that seemed pertinent to my situation. I had an unplanned stay with Anne and Michael, the parents of an old school friend of mine, which happened to be en route – the first of many such encounters – and then a rest day with Pip and Ben in the south of France after a week.

I had two friends, Jack and Jilly, fly out to ride with me for three days. I thought maybe this trip, like many unconven-tional decisions in life, could be a useful gauge of friendship and priorities; both theirs and mine. Jack, Jilly and I hit the coast, swam excitedly in the sea and shared bottles of wine. It felt rather more like a holiday than a grand adventure. And then we bid each other farewell in the knowledge that our next encounter was a date far away in the future.

I rode across Italy, stayed with three interesting and kind people, Marco, Simone and Luca: a dog walker, a rock musician and an animal-loving chess maestro. I found abandoned farmhouses to sleep in when it was raining, fixed mechanical issues and left superfluous bits of kit at a bus stop. I revelled in sitting in the sun with an espresso at little cafes. The weather was agreeable, the days were long, the miles were big and my morale was high.

Having been politely removed from Monaco by the police after trying to cycle the Formula One circuit, I was then politely removed from Venice for riding my bike around when I knew full well it was not permitted. It was emancipating being a nobody, an outsider, and exercising my little tendencies towards rule-breaking here and there.

My family was amazed at the speed I was going when, within a few weeks, I had shared pictures of flags from France, Italy, Slovenia, Croatia, Hungary and Romania. My mind was running in sixth gear to absorb and process everything I saw and experienced. Already there had been moments of frustration, humour, blissful calm and curiosity. I had been stopped several times by drivers, enthusiastic about what I was doing, wanting a selfie and to give me food and water before driving on. Those small moments stuck with me. When spending so much time alone every day, exasperated by an inability to communicate your thoughts properly with people, the positive, or occasionally negative, encounters whir around the mind hour after hour.

In a small cafe in Slovenia, the waitress, Jarja, and I got chatting as my sweaty cap and sunglasses sat on the table. By now I was accustomed to being an odd addition to social settings. Jarja was a handbag designer, working here part-time before crossing the Austrian border every few weeks to sell her designs. I told her about my trip, where I had come from and where I was going. Without even a hint, she made me a pizza and brought over a juice and another coffee. Jarja believed she needed to do what she could to help me along the way.

In her words, 'I like to think kindness comes around to those who give it out, so that's how I have tried to live my life.'

After the gorgeous lakes and mountains of Slovenia, there came the putrid road-killed dogs of Hungary before the horse-drawn carts and wacky architecture of Romania. There were storms, thunder, lightning, hail and rainbows. There was the extraordinary detour I took to ride up the Transfăgărășan Highway in Transylvania. Built in the 1970s, six million kilograms of dynamite were used to make the road crossing the highest peaks in the country. Twenty miles and 1,500 metres of lung-bursting pedalling through the mist up what Jeremy Clarkson called the most amazing road he'd ever seen. Switchbacks, steep valleys, green forests and a nerve-shredding, brake-burning descent down the other side ensued. I had to earn the views but the ten-year wait to ride the road had been worth it.

---

Charlotte flew out to Bucharest to spend the weekend with me. We had been dating a few months and things accelerated fast in the knowledge I was leaving for an indefinite amount of time – hardly the foundations of a stable relationship. I saw her the day before I pedalled away from home and we parted amicably. But after a few weeks apart, we began to miss each other. I gave her a location and a date; she gave me motivation to ensure I arrived when I said I would.

It was a lovely weekend of street music, good food, wine and romance tinged with a sense of personal guilt. I had little financial flexibility, but worse than that, I felt bad she had flown to eastern Europe to see me when I was distracted by where I was going rather than where I was and I realised that, come Sunday night, our paths would be heading in very different directions. Charlotte was aware of it, consciously or unconsciously. And I knew she knew.

We parted, again. This time, it was conclusive. I didn't know how I would feel upon returning, or indeed when that would be. In my view, the journey I had embarked upon and a relationship were not compatible. My head was somewhere in Central Asia; it had to be. If I was not going to commit unequivocally and embrace the rare opportunity of this trip then what was the point? If I rode half-heartedly in the knowledge of an alternative reality at home, I would either not want to depart, call it quits halfway or resent the journey.

As Charlotte and I headed our separate ways, we both knew, as independent spirits, we would be okay.

I rode away and thought about something she had said: 'You're going to have to grow up at some stage, Geordie. Just not yet. And you wouldn't be you if you did. Remember also, when all this has gone, you must be left with something or someone that will make you happy and make ordinary life seem extraordinary still. Bike safely and have the most amazing adventure.'

One of my favourite childhood stories was that of Peter Pan – the boy who wouldn't grow up. Charlotte made me think about my stage of life and whether I had accepted it or not. I was not twenty-three anymore and fresh out of university. I was no longer wide-eyed and ignorant about the world. My peer group of friends were getting engaged, married and having children, settling down with stable jobs and mortgages. They certainly weren't sacking it all in and gallivanting around the world on two wheels.

On a deeper level, maybe this whole trip was about escapism and a fear of settling down. Maybe there was a simmering apprehension about the life I could foresee up ahead and this ride was an easy and justifiable way to delay that existence. I knew, amongst other things, that this was one of the reasons I was here. Then there was the other perspective: that this trip was a final chance at freedom before accepting, perhaps embracing, adulthood proper.

The premise of the trip, the urge to leave one's home alone in search of faraway places, is a selfish one. There could be selfless by-products, of course, but the core motivation has to be internal or the incentive to ride every day would be insufficient. Splitting with Charlotte made me confront my own flaws once again. I knew I would have thousands of miles and hours to deliberate over this in the months ahead.

---

Bulgaria was unsettling as I came to terms with what I was leaving behind. It was the location where I reflected upon another link in the chain of stability that I had let go. I also viewed it as a means to an end – a transitory place before I got to Turkey and the real goal of Istanbul. But despite a night of getting assaulted by an army of ants, which tore holes in my tent, I became unexpectedly fond of the place. I disconnected from the Internet, rode beautiful forested mountain passes, wild camped every night, watched serene sunsets, drank tea and read books on philosophy. It was a reflective and slightly melancholic interlude but important; a chance to accept rather than regret. Nature, as she often does, provided stillness and perspective.

I then prepared for Turkey where things would seriously change. I needed a visa and was no longer able to use my UK SIM card. I was certainly out of western Europe in terms of culture, language, religion and currency.

And then there was cycling into Istanbul.

I had read about this and spoken to friends who had ridden into the city but, like many things, it has to be done to be appreciated. Initially what struck me was the sheer distance from the built-up outskirts to the city centre. Two lanes turned into four. Four lanes into six. Two tiers of roads. Six lanes heading in the opposite direction. Rain lashing down. Police sirens, car horns, swerving buses, a narrowing hard shoulder, no hard shoulder. Sweaty inclines evolving into steep 50-mph descents. It was a case of holding on, keeping a straight line and hoping nobody did anything rash in front. It was chaotic, laughably so, as I just kept spinning the wheels and hoping.

Finally, I hauled my bike up the fiendishly steep side streets and knew I was in Istanbul proper as famous mosques and iconic buildings emerged either side. It was an important juncture. Setting off with gusto for the road is one thing but following through is another altogether. The city represented the crossing of Europe and, as such, was in itself a legitimate achievement: cycling across a continent.

I had said farewell to my sisters in London and my mum in Hampshire, but my dad and stepmother flew out to see me in Istanbul. It was a good excuse for them to visit the city but they also sensed the significance. We had an enjoyable few days exploring as tourists and soaking up the atmosphere but I was physically tired, having cycled almost 4,000 miles across Europe in thirty-seven days. I was relieved and grateful to be with people who trusted and loved me. The unknowns ahead, namely isolation and winter, worried me. They detected, as Charlotte had in Bucharest, that part of my brain was somewhere else, somewhere months and many miles down the road.

I was reluctant to leave the familiar but had to push on.

I rode inland and over mountains before moving speedily towards the Black Sea. I had to maintain momentum. Winter was approaching; it concerned and spurred me on in equal measure. I rode into Georgia and took a detour up over the Goderdzi Pass. I was given warnings by locals as the tarmac turned to roadworks, and the rocks to mud. People motioned that heavy winds were coming and encouraged me to stay with them but onwards I ascended into the mist. The temperature dropped as visibility was heavily reduced and my clothes became saturated with sweat. I reached the top with my lights on as darkness fell before entering a cafe and being greeted by Nargizi and her husband, Otali.

Nargizi immediately showed compassion, dried my clothes on the stove, gave me tea to drink and delicious Georgian cheese and bread to eat before offering me shelter for the night. I noticed several people had written letters on the wall of her cafe expressing their thanks for her hospitality so I wrote a little note and pinned it up alongside that of another cyclist who appeared to have experienced similar kindness in a not dissimilar situation.

*An unexpected traffic jam on the Goderdzi Pass*

I then stayed with an army friend, Lauren, in Tbilisi. I was grateful for a break and temporary respite. We went to a wonderful mountain film festival together but otherwise it was a chance to read, write, relax and do yoga. Alarmingly, beyond Tbilisi I had no other checkpoints for five months until I reached Southeast Asia. Lauren's apartment was my final safety net.

On I went, out of Georgia and into Azerbaijan, where I was met with remarkable levels of curiosity, from children especially, who would walk up to smile and wave at me while I sat in bus stops. Despite wanting to savour where I was, I also had to plan my next move. There are three ways to negotiate the Caspian Sea from Azerbaijan: head south through Iran, north through Russia or take a cargo ship straight across. All three are logistically challenging but two of them were not diplomatically possible so I chose the final option.

I made it to Alat – about forty miles south of Baku – and prepared for an exasperating ordeal at the hands of the Azerbaijan Caspian Shipping Company. The ferry timetable itself was a confusion of whispers, rumours and sudden, frantic action. Darkness was setting in on night three when a man poked his head around the cafe door and said, 'Kazakhstan, we go.'

Giddy excitement ensued. We were on the boat and heading for Central Asia. As so often happens, however, within a few hours the winds grew too high for us to continue and the anchor went down. We were stranded once more.

I was fortunate to be joined by a few other travellers with whom I could laugh at our surreal situation. A pair of German graduates, Alex and Rapha, were exploring Central Asia in a battered van. And a lovely British couple, Jack and Helen, were travelling the world together after having quit their jobs in London in their thirties. Together we endured our windowless, airless cabins, ate rice, chicken and stale bread, and played draughts with the truck drivers as we got going again. One of the latter claimed to be the Kyrgyz champion, and having seen the speed at which he played, it was hard to disagree. The nights of camping on concrete in the rain at the ferry terminal had made me tetchy; I just wanted to keep moving. But the imposed break was probably a positive. We could chat as five Europeans about our hopes, experiences and expectations of what lay ahead.

We formed three groups, with three different modes of transport, each understanding the other but with a strong proclivity towards their own method of seeing the world. I was partially envious that the others had someone to share the road with but also happy to be alone. I wanted the desert. I craved the isolation.

---

The Turkish, Kazakh and Kyrgyz truck drivers on the ferry were in little rush so I rolled my bike to the front of the queue upon arrival. My passport and visa were scrutinised by the border guard. He left his cubicle and I sat down while my details were processed. I wasn't expecting it to be quick; it rarely was. Another border guard joined me for a smoke. We could not communicate but he was keen to prod my bike a bit, smile a toothy grin at my Highland cow mascot, squeeze the tyres and test the weight of everything I owned.

I wondered what was beyond the heavy gates. It felt like the portal to a real adventure – to mainland Asia, with a history, culture and language far removed from those of my own European home. My visa and passport were finally returned. The official opened the gate and I heard the reassuringly familiar sound of my sandals clipping into pedals. Into Kazakhstan I went.

# PART II

---

# FREEDOM

*The gladdest moment in human life, methinks, is a departure
into unknown lands.*

— Richard Burton

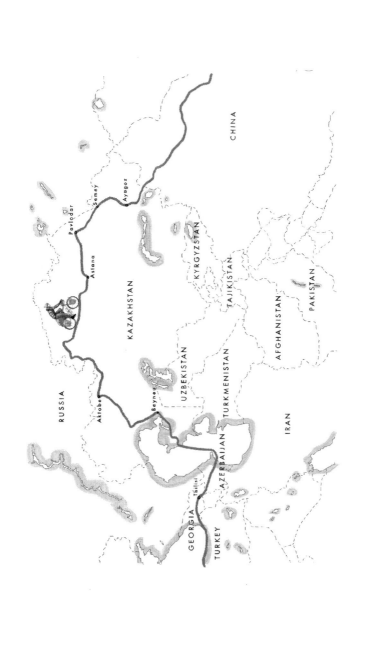

# 1.

Part of me felt like a naughty child when I began cycling north after my left turn at the T-junction. The decision was irresponsible but irresistibly appealing. Cycle tourers tend to cross Europe in their own way but all end up with the same dilemma on the western edge of Asia. Assuming the aim was to end in east Asia, in terms of time and distance my decision made no sense. In terms of expected weather and remoteness, it didn't make any sense, either. But somehow, to me, there was sense in the senselessness. I did not want to continue hopping borders for the next few months, notionally engaging with a region only to part from it again soon after. I wanted to engage with a place and understand it properly.

A satellite image on Google Maps showed me everything I needed to know. Rather than the greenery which had dominated my 4,000 miles through Europe, a khaki-coloured shading covered the next 6,000 miles of Central Asia. Rolling green hills, bright flowers and verdant forests were in the past. There would no longer be cows and sheep, but camels and horses amidst the brown dullness of the autumnal

Kazakh Steppe. It all seemed a great adventure; the wider task too overwhelming to take in.

As I moved further into Kazakhstan and the human company dwindled, I sought strength and relatability in the animals I encountered. The herds of wild horses with dust thrown up behind them moved as a collective, seeming so liberated and pure. They always moved together; a lone Steppe horse never crossed my path. They flicked their tails on each other to ward away flies. When a solitary cyclist passed by, they fled as a group. When the vicious, unimpeded winds ripped across the barren landscape, they stood together, as penguins do, taking turns to do duty on the outside of the group before sheltering within. In the army you are trained to look out for others, to place the collective goal above the individual and work together. I respected the horses' teamwork but felt at odds with it, being a lone traveller in this foreign land.

Camels had a stoicism about them I felt more akin to. Often they were part of a wider caravan but they moved at their own pace. When the winds increased, the temperatures decreased and the ground hardened, the camels didn't grow flustered. They had seen all this before and nothing fazed them, secure as they were in the knowledge that they could sustain themselves for days on end without external support. I never knew where they came from or where they were going but they were always on a journey somewhere, always moving but never rushing, indifferent to the world around them.

As I cycled past they would occasionally stop and their munching would temporarily desist. Their glances and body language said enough; it was a look of intrigue, like that of a hardened mountaineer seeing a young pretender rush at the base of a climb. He says nothing but knows everything. He's seen it before, likely he's been that ambitious young man himself. Internally he wishes the young climber well and hopes he might also learn a tough but valuable lesson in the process. He knows the pace cannot be sustained and he's unprepared but knowledge is often gained through experience. Our experiences are what test us, harden us and mould our view of the world.

For the camels, experience was everything. The hot dry summer was as strenuous as the bitter cold winter. I thought I knew what lay ahead, but not really. I knew the land would be sparse, the winds would be strong and the autumn would end, but I was yet to experience it. The camels knew, and their look told me so. I liked to think they were quietly nodding in approval, wishing me luck and hoping I would send a postcard when I was safely out the other side.

*Finding strength and relatability from unexpected sources*

I analysed the map ahead and knew my first significant stop where I could find a bed and shower was several weeks away in a city called Aktobe. My rough planning gave me a 1,000-mile route skirting the Russian border. It followed the only main road and was suggested by the truck drivers and locals I'd spoken to. Google Maps – a dangerous planning tool with little regard for cycling capability – provided an alternative that would cut off 350 miles prior to Aktobe. This shortcut *could* save time but came with significant risks from suspect terrain and minimal support. I felt the adventurous spirit again: I took the shortcut.

Almost immediately, the tarmac was replaced by a rutted dirt track. I bounced along for hours, feeling chirpy – again, a naughty kid on a silly adventure. I could hear Dorothy, my sturdy British bike and only current companion, bounce along beneath me. She also enjoyed the contrast, a chance to show what she was capable of.

Dorothy was a slightly rogue second-hand eBay purchase. I was reassured by the fact that the previous owner, Dean, had a meticulously laid-out garage containing several other bikes and a glistening car in the driveway. He was a man who clearly took care of things. I trusted Dean would have taken care of Dorothy; I hoped so anyway. Her biggest test was yet to come.

As the day waned, my shadows increased in length and my energy levels decreased. A slight depression in the ground a few hundred metres off the track was the best camp I could muster that evening. I wasn't overly concerned; I hadn't seen or heard a vehicle since I'd turned off, and the darkness would conceal my presence until I was ready to move again in the morning.

I was now fully accustomed to my routine: I put up my tent, boiled water, cooked noodles, made a cup of tea and sat outside in a jacket to watch the sun setting on this sweeping landscape. I had been to big deserts, hot and cold – the Sahara and Antarctica – but this was different again. The Steppe was austere and uninviting yet absorbing – there was a kind of beauty in its blandness.

The lack of distractions on the horizon ensured a compulsive focus on the conditions overhead. I had a sense things were turning unfavourable when, for the first time in a few weeks in Kazakhstan, clouds dominated the sky. Spend enough time looking at and interpreting the sky and you begin to trust your instincts. It was autumn and the nights were getting chilly.

Up until this point, I had been cycling mainly in a T-shirt, shorts, sandals and my trusty cap. As I ventured further north, however, the shorts gave way to trousers, the T-shirt to a long-sleeved top, often with a thin rain jacket on top, and the increasingly suspect tan lines from my sandals were covered up by socks. Socks and sandals are a much-maligned fashion statement to a Brit but, as a travelling cyclist, the combination provided all the convenience and practicality I needed with a hint of self-amusement thrown into the mix.

The clouds transitioned from puffy white cumuli to general bleakness. I knew what was coming. The word 'petrichor' came to mind – the term used to describe the distinct scent of rain in the air, specifically the name of an oil given off by the earth before rain begins to fall. On dusty tracks, rainfall causes firm soil to quickly moisten and acts like a vacuum for a tyre, sucking it in from all sides. Each pedal stroke demands added power and achieves less distance. The contours on the track become harder to identify and make the bike prone to sliding sideways. Speed and momentum declines. Mud was splatting everywhere, I was making little progress, the rain was tiresome and my body temperature cooling. I weighed up the merit of ploughing on versus sitting it out.

One lesson from my army training at Sandhurst went through my head: that of compounding failure. A simple idea but so applicable to so many aspects of our lives – relationships, jobs, sport, politics. At what stage do we put the brakes on a particular course and redirect, even if it means retracing our own steps?

This was one of those moments. There were no cars and no shelter. I had ridden a few hundred miles along a random track and was moving nowhere fast. I was compounding failure. Perhaps even the decision at the T-junction at Beyneu had been an error and I was pursuing a foolish route, now simply for the sake of my own pride.

At some point, however, you just have to put your faith in something and make a decision. When Joe Simpson escaped from the crevasse he had fallen into in South America, instead of climbing up, he rappelled down. His options had been limited and he had made a choice. Clearly my current situation was not as drastic but the principle was worth bearing in mind. I pedalled on, getting wetter and muddier as I moved over the sodden ground.

Finding a camping spot was theoretically easy given the vast expanse of emptiness either side of the road. In practice, however, it proved rather more tricky. The strong winds meant I needed a physical barrier to provide protection. Tents are resilient but there was no point in adding extra layers of risk with something so integral to my own safety.

Good tent placement is essential. Ideally you need visibility of routes in and out, protection both from the elements and from potential intruders. Ideally you want good communication, accessibility and a water supply as well. Safety and security are the big ones. Your aim is to stay covert. Wind direction matters because, firstly, a tent has structural strengths and weaknesses and, secondly, you do not want wind driving into your porch when you're trying to cook.

With saturated ground either side of me and foul weather, camping on the Steppe would be a challenge I was not seeking. I kept telling myself the same thing again and again, namely, 'Something will emerge,' because, quite honestly, in the absence of anything else, I only had hope. So on we went, sliding and hoping. The music in my ears became less serene and more aggressive – did I adjust the music to my mood, or did the music adjust my mood? When I knew what was ahead, I could tweak the playlist to suit the ambiance I wanted. This was not a time for self-reflection and worldly musings, but rather for a focused attempt on making progress.

Not always, but sometimes, one's faith is rewarded. In the words from *The Alchemist* by Paulo Coelho, 'When you want something, all the universe conspires in helping you to achieve it.' While I don't wholly agree with the sentiment, I do believe that the pursuit of our goals, if done with perseverance, openness and compassion, can lead to the most rewarding of outcomes.

The rain eased as the light began to fade. I had accepted the prospect of a wet night in my tent; it was nothing new. But then, a few hundred metres off the track, a building loomed into view. It was abandoned and totally isolated but it was shelter. I wearily hauled my bike through the mud, having given up trying to stay clean and dry.

I peered anxiously around the house. Tattered clothes lay in the corner of a few rooms. I noted smashed walls, split floorboards, no lightbulbs and no windows. The staircase lay broken leaving a gaping hole in the floor above. A smell of dampness lingered – the splintered roof provided only notional protection from the elements. But it was shelter. It was the most shelter I had had thus far in Kazakhstan and, other than the Caspian Sea crossing, the only shelter since Georgia. It would do just fine. A little sanctuary. A dingy, dirty sanctuary but a sanctuary indeed.

I stripped off, replacing my sodden clothes with dry ones which had survived the downpour. A wet wipe wash and some chocolate raised morale. There was no phone reception but I had music, I always had music. In what appeared to have been the living room in this abandoned house, I danced around with my headtorch, acknowledging that a passer-by or extraterrestrial being would question my sanity. I was, however, dry and safe after having completed another tough day. It was reason enough to be chirpy and to hop on the bike again in the morning to see what the next day would bring.

An airport arrival in a foreign city is a shock. We go from our own norm to the abnormal. We go from being a local to a foreigner, while others aboard the flight go from being a foreigner to a local. Mid-flight, while one person edges further away from their country, another edges closer. But the arrival is sudden; there is no gradual change of scenery, culture or language.

Travelling by bike is at the other end of the spectrum; differences emerge slowly. Great mountain ranges appear far in the distance as specks at the edge of our sight. Gradually, day after day, they emerge into view with increased clarity. Rather than a vague outline, individual peaks, gullies and cols appear. Their magnitude is heightened as the daunting prospect of crossing over them becomes a realistic possibility.

On a bike, you're constantly analysing the near, middle and far ground. What is right in front of you dominates the immediacy of your thoughts: potholes, debris, dirt, roadkill. The middle ground is where our short-term focus becomes active: the next bend in the road, notable features ahead, the next hill or cars in the distance. The far ground is where the goal-setting part of our brain is zoned in. That gives us a further focus and a wider ambition.

The very idea of pedalling across Europe and Asia is so daunting, it might become overwhelming. As with any large ambition, it is necessary to break it down into manageable chunks to make it achievable. I reduced it by saying I wanted to get to Monaco, then Bucharest, Istanbul, Tbilisi and Kazakhstan. Then it was China, Vietnam and the rest of Southeast Asia before Singapore. I would rarely make precise plans more than a couple of days in advance, yet I planned months ahead to give me something to aim towards.

Understandably, friends back home asked how I funded such a trip. I had been extremely frugal in my final six months in the army, cancelled my outgoings and sold many of my belongings. I saved enough money to make the trip possible *if* I lived a certain way on the road. Cycling from London to Istanbul I spent about £300. It was what other people might spend on a sofa, a new phone, tyres for their car, a TV or a new washing machine. Similarly, my expenses between London and China would be £1,000 – for some, the same as their rent or a new laptop.

Having saved money for the trip, I could have travelled more lavishly but only for a short stint. In order to achieve my ambition, I had to alter my habits and shift my priorities. While preparing for the trip, I had questioned the value of a meal out or cocktail at a bar in London given what it could provide when I was away. I had the same approach while riding. A night in a hotel costing £20 was not worth it; that money could enable me to survive a week. Instead I camped and cooked out of one pot on a stove most nights.

I did not have the finances to live in luxury on the road. I was clear in my priorities. I constantly deliberated about what the 'future me' would be glad I had done and what I would regret not having done. I knew that, in the years to come, the memories and lessons learned from the trip would far outweigh the temporary discomforts.

---

Sometimes, faced with difficulties, I grew frustrated. The lack of speed, headwinds and damage being done to the bike received the brunt of my monologues. As much as I tried to deflect the blame to Google Maps or the Kazakh government, it was a defence mechanism; the reality was, everything came down to my decisions. Had I been with someone else, I would likely have stuck to my original plan and would now be further south. Even if we had ventured north, few others would have been idiotic enough to take the unnecessary shortcut I had.

I could have just taken the safer alternative. But that's why it was invigorating. I knew I would look back fondly on the mud-sliding and the anxiety of knowing I was stranded if something went wrong. I knew a long stint without other cyclists and without showering was, in an odd way, something to be positive about. It was both foolish and thrilling.

The rainstorm had thankfully passed. The single track transitioned into a delta of alternatives. As with a flow chart, I would ride along one dusty track which would eventually descend into the 'unworkable' category. And then the flow chart would stem out again and give me a number of other options. There was a difference, of course, which was that a flow chart leads to a variety of outcomes whereas I hoped for only one: the rejoining of a more significant road at the small town of Kandyagash. Realistically, there were no alternatives as venturing off route was not possible. Some way or another, regardless of the awkwardness involved and the time it took me, I would get there.

The flat terrain ensured that increasing winds would stunt my progress. The dust and sand whirled around me, restricting my vision and coarsening the back of my throat. I could see the changing colour of my clothes and feel the matted texture of my hair. It had been several weeks since my last shower.

Occasionally, across the hundred-metre width of alternative routes, I would see a dust cloud in the distance and a car or lorry would pass in the opposite direction. Rarely would we have picked the same track, each just planning a few metres ahead, so we passed by without a word. These rare encounters gave me reassurance – should a disaster occur, there might be someone who could help.

This continued for hundreds of miles and several days. The distance covered was dramatically below what I had been clocking up but I expected nothing different here and had prepared accordingly with extra food and water bottles strapped to my panniers. At times, I would remind myself that this was what life was all about, or at least the life I was currently enveloped in: adventure and exploration. Feeling vulnerable and anxious about what *could* happen was part of the adventure; the security of knowing all possible outcomes had disappeared.

While bouncing along uncomfortably, my mind was often occupied by various 'what ifs'. I had no phone reception to research bike shops, restaurants or garages. I had a basic selection of bike repair parts and medical equipment. Barring a serious drama, both could be utilised to seek some solution to a predicament. As I had learned on expeditions over the years, nothing creates resourcefulness like necessity. When there is no alternative and nobody else around, you are solely reliant on finding your own way out of the problem.

---

Prior to arriving in Kazakhstan, I knew little about the country. I recognised the flag, I was familiar with their cycling team, Astana, and a few of their sporting superstars, namely the boxer Gennady Golovkin and Olympic gold medal-winning cyclist Alexander Vinokourov. I knew it was the home country of the fictitious character Borat, something I was obviously not keen to discuss with the locals, and was aware of its natural resources, namely oil and gas. Wild horses and its history as part of the Soviet Union rounded off what was the broadest of brush strokes.

From Genghis Khan's Mongol Empire to modern-day Kazakhstan, the horse has been highly valued and significant. In Britain, horses are used for sporting and leisure activities but little else. In Kazakhstan, and much of Central Asia and Mongolia, horses represent far more. Indeed, some say the Kazakhs were the first people to domesticate and ride horses.

Horse riding is a large part of Kazakh culture. One of its most famous manifestations is the sport known as *kyz kuu*, which literally translates as 'girl chasing'. The game, which can be simplified to a kiss chase on horseback, combines elements of romance and tradition. A woman sets off on a horse at a gallop. After a small delay, a man, also on horseback, chases after her. The aim is for the man to catch the girl and kiss her while both are still at full kilter: a sign of his victory. If the female rider gets to the finishing line first, she turns around and chases the man back towards the start. While riding she tries to come closer to the male rider and beat him with the whip she's holding. This marks her victory.

Considering Brits chase a rolling cheese down a hill in Gloucestershire and host the World Stone Skimming Championships, I had only praise for *kyz kuu* – its uniqueness and history made me happy.

Giant statues of Kazakhs on horseback occasionally appeared along my way, dominating the view for miles around. Sometimes it was an armoured man thrusting a spear downwards while his perfectly maintained charger remained poised beneath him. On other occasions, it appeared to be a returning general, fresh from a successful campaign, with a gold tip to his helmet and spear. A final theme was the statesman waving to a crowd with a softer hat from atop an unarmoured and slender mare. Always male and always on horseback.

---

Aktobe was the first urban area I experienced in Kazakhstan; after the simplicity of the Steppe it provided a cultural shock. Upon arriving, I found a cheap hostel – the first night of accommodation I had paid for since leaving the UK – and showered, several times. I'd grown so accustomed to my own skin tone and personal appearance, I was oblivious to the accumulated dust, dirt and grime. My basic wet wipe washing kept the essentials clean but the majority of my body was thankful for the upgrade.

Though I was content with my own company, I remained keen to speak to people when I connected back to the world. I was delighted to hear of a friend's recent engagement and my own morale was raised by her vociferous praise for how far I had gone. I didn't want to study maps too much; I could not help but see the chasms of space between where I was and where I needed to go. However, seeing the dot located where it was and listening to my friend down the phone did give me a pleasing boost.

I was independent but the kindness of strangers had been pretty constant since the start of the trip. People I met put me in touch with friends or friends of friends at different places further down the road; total strangers acted instinctively to assist me on numerous occasions. The latter experiences never failed to be truly humbling and were greatly appreciated. From Jarja and Luca buying me dinner in Slovenian and Italian cafes respectively, to Mesut and Bahri doing the same in Turkey, people with whom I had no prior connection – and would likely have no future connection with either – showed a willingness to help. Often we had no common tongue, leaving only our gestures and body language to convey our thoughts and emotions. Other times, the simplest of words in another language went far to showing the respect I had for the culture of where I was.

Part of the appeal of my route was that it provided an opportunity to embrace and understand a place I had previously known little about. It was a chance to alter the preconceptions I had and develop more specific knowledge. Any elongated stint in a country will enable this to happen but travelling across a country by bike, visiting deprived rural areas, small towns and modern capitals, gives a different perspective.

In the afternoon, I was in a small supermarket buying essential supplies: staples like noodles and porridge, as well as things I was grateful to see again and stock up on, such as fresh fruit and peanut butter. Typically confused at the till with my limited Russian, I was grateful when the man behind me acted as a translator with impeccable English. It transpired that Yerlan was a school teacher in the city and he persuaded me to stay an extra twenty-four hours and give a few talks the following day. I was initially hesitant to take a rest day but it felt both necessary and important to do so. Chance encounters, with that delicious element of serendipity, are something to be embraced.

Fast-forward to the following morning and I found myself being interviewed on Kazakh national television and giving several talks to the students and teachers of a small school. I've given a huge number of school talks over the years and believe enormously in their value, having had my interest piqued by various inspirational people when I was younger. It was something I was happy to do and if the result was positive PR for the school and a different perspective for the students and teachers, then it was a win-win.

Beyond the talks, the greatest outcome of the day were the conversations I had and the exchange of ideas. Kazakhstan only gained independence from the Soviet Union in 1991. As a result, the country's identity was still being shaped under their first president, Nursultan Nazarbayev, who holds the title 'Leader of the Nation'. The teachers wanted to know about my perception of their country while I was interested in what they thought about the UK. The contrast between our nations and cultures generated some of the most interesting discussions I had on the entire trip. Above all, it was fascinating to see how the vast socioeconomic differences often overshadowed similar values and priorities about work, family and community.

Yerlan's invitation was not for personal gain but rather to help others and a lunch we shared exemplified that. On the menu were two Central Asian staples: *beshbarmak* and *kumis*.

The term *beshbarmak* means 'five fingers' because the dish is traditionally eaten with one's hands and is about sharing and openness with the others present. Basically, it is a noodle and meat dish with minimal ingredients: dough, meat, onions, broth, some spices and oil or butter. The cooking process, presentation and taste is of great importance.

Nomadic Kazakhs were naturally constrained by the environment in which they lived and worked. Their reliance upon their animals for survival is reflected in their food, which revolves around meat and dairy. Although *beshbarmak* is seen as the national dish of Kazakhstan, it is usually reserved for special occasions such as weddings, funerals and holidays or to honour a visiting guest.

Most foreigners sample *beshbarmak* at a restaurant, as I did with Yerlan and Nursultan, an intelligent and well-travelled student who joined us. I felt privileged that they viewed my presence as a worthwhile justification for eating the dish that carries with it Kazakhstan's nomadic identity.

*Kumis*, on the other hand, went down with rather less pleasure but with an equal amount of curiosity. As with *beshbarmak*, it derives from the nomadic Kazakh culture and uses natural produce from the animals that for so long were essential for their survival. *Kumis* is therefore an important part of the nation's culinary history.

I was open to the idea, of course, but remained wary when I saw Yerlan and Nursultan look over with raised eyes as I held up my bowl. Usually served chilled, *kumis* is made by fermenting raw, unpasteurised mare's milk over a period of

hours or days, with regular stirring or churning, and is traditionally sipped out of a small, handle-less, bowl-shaped cup
or saucer called a *piyala*. While similar to the more agreeable-
tasting *kefir*, *kumis* has a uniquely sharp, sour bite and is
mildly alcoholic. The lunch of *kumis* and *beshbarmak* spoke
volumes beyond the meal itself.

*Kumis for Yerlan, Nursultan and I in Aktobe*

I was due to leave Aktobe in the morning and had been
grateful for the break. My body and mind needed the pause
before progressing.

It was now approaching the end of October and the temperature was falling – not alarming yet but noticeable. The
mercury was only going to drop further between here and
Astana (in March 2019, Astana was renamed Nur-Sultan after
the departing Kazakh president, Nursultan Nazarbayev), the
capital of Kazakhstan and my next stop. A little preparation
was therefore necessary.

Accordingly, Yerlan and I went whizzing around the Aktobe
shopping malls, Yerlan acting as a gracious intermediary

explaining to sales assistants what I needed. I love cross-country skiing but, on this occasion, seeing skis stacked up alongside woolly hats, socks and gloves in outdoor stores hardly filled me with enthusiasm. This was not the time for full winter preparation but I needed a few extras to ensure I could cover the 1,000 miles to Astana in decent order.

I was about to buy a pair of gloves when Yerlan handed me some money to pay for them. I refused; it was a lovely gesture but it was not his role to finance my solo venture. He explained with all the kindheartedness in his character that it was not his money, but rather that the teachers at the school had pooled together to buy something to help me. I did not know what to say but Yerlan insisted he buy the gloves as a way of saying thank you and good luck both from him and his school. I humbly accepted.

As Yerlan and I parted ways, I was grateful our paths had crossed. His warmth and generosity of spirit had come exactly when I needed it. I knew those memories would be important as I continued. We exchanged numbers and he said if anything were to happen or I needed help during the remainder of my journey through Kazakhstan, I should let him know and he would ensure help came my way.

I wondered whether someone in the UK would have done the same for a foreign traveller. I wondered whether I would have done the same. I asked Yerlan why he had decided to help me. He quoted a Kazakh saying that translated as, 'Fortune is good to him who knows how to make good use of it.' Yerlan was a kind-hearted man who wanted to share good with others.

## 2.

Deserts, always deserts. So many of my favourite authors and travellers found something profound in the desert. What was it in those vast expanses of unforgiving terrain that spoke so powerfully? What quixotic yearning drives people to seek understanding in those lands? In his novella *Le Petit Prince*, Antoine de Saint-Exupéry wrote, 'I have always loved the desert… You see nothing. You hear nothing. And yet something shines, something sings in that silence…'

The desert, untamed and unruly like a mountain, forces man to reflect. The wildness and uncontrollability demand deference and respect. Conditions can change from convivial to chaotic in an instant. Just as climbers can find themselves stranded, alone and exposed after a change of opinion from Mother Nature, travellers in the desert are also at the mercy of the elements.

Life on the road had become my world; my bike merely the mechanism by which to experience it. Eliminating the need for navigation was a blessing. From Aktobe to Astana, there was only one feasible route, with no realistic turnoff. I had nowhere to stay. I had no time agenda. I could consciously try to be present in my own mind, understand where I was and the choices I made. My mind was both sedentary and alert, drifting from the past to the future and sometimes finding a peacefulness in the present. On previous expeditions, there had always been a teammate next to me. Now, I could camp in the wild, look ahead and see both the wholeness of life and total freedom – everything and nothing.

On the Steppe, the sky was vast, the setting immense. On cloudless days, the sole presence in the deep blue vista was the sun, radiant and pure. All around was open land with nothing to impede one's vision. To my left was Russia, at times barely a metre away. There was no obvious border and certainly no change in the surroundings, just the Steppe. To my right, thousands of miles of Kazakhstan unfurled.

Every morning, I woke at sunrise and peeked my head outside the tent. The landscape remained unchanged for miles around but the colours altered with the position of the sun and I felt as impressed with where I was as when I had wriggled into my sleeping bag not long before. I cooked porridge, added honey, ate and then packed up my tent, making sure no trace of my presence was left behind. Another temporary home for the night, another unique moment I hoped not to forget. I clipped on my panniers, strapped down my main bag with a few bungees, and a new day began.

So much was the same, day after day, crossing this vast land-scape, and yet there were always welcome differences. The temperature or wind direction might alter slightly, there were tweaks in the road surface and changes in distance from where I had been and where I was going. There was even excitement in, or as a result of, the monotony.

In Aktobe I had messaged a few friends a picture of the landscape I had been in. They commented simply, 'Looks bleak.' I was so immersed in where I was, so absorbed by my surroundings, the two words bothered me. For me, the Steppe had become far from bleak; on the contrary, it was beautiful. My friends could not see the beauty in the barrenness, or understand how the emptiness served to liberate my spirit.

Some days, the cloud formations dominated the world as far as I could see. When clouds were present, I could be distracted by the psychological phenomenon called 'pareidolia'. This causes people to see patterns in random stimuli – in this case, I was seeing objects in clouds. It was a simple mechanism to distract the mind and allow it to wander.

There were no hills in the distance to provide points of reference. There was rarely a bend in the road to aim towards. The flatness of the landscape distorted my mind and confused my sense of progress. A rare cluster of abandoned buildings or trees might emerge at the limit of my vision but nothing was visible on the map. Aspects of the Steppe were a delusionary form of purgatory, enough to send one insane with warped perceptions of gradients, distance and space.

The wind somehow blocked my progress; it never seemed to blow from behind. The route ahead always appeared uphill. I would then sit on the side of the road, sip my water, and look back to where I had come from: it was also always uphill. Progress appeared minimal because for long periods nothing changed; but then, quite suddenly, the hours of effort would be rewarded by a diminishing number on the road signs for Astana.

My animal companions, the camels and horses so numerous in the southwest, became a rarity. The eagles, so famous and iconic in Kazakhstan, were fewer but now I longed for their graceful presence. They would occasionally appear, floating above, scanning the ground for signs of life in order to sustain their own. To me, they felt like watchful protectors gliding with the winds as I pedalled below. And then they were gone, sharply cornering away, and I was alone again.

Population density and traffic were also significantly reduced. Occasionally trucks passed by on this logistical artery but the noticeable proportion of cars were heading in the opposite direction, escaping the impending doom of winter brutality while I was heading straight into it. Yerlan had informed me that such a migration was the norm in autumn. Mattresses and containers were strapped on top of vehicles as families doggedly covered the necessary miles towards friends and relatives in another part of the country.

---

It is rare we get the chance to reverse the trend of constant connectivity and reduce ourselves to just being. I had weeks with minimal scenic distractions but, crucially, two key elements: time and space.

The need for self-awareness and personal space – physical and mental – has been, and remains, a key part of my life. Yoga and meditation have been important pillars since I was a teenager. As I've got older, I have seen how the free time I had, for example, at university has been replaced by other commitments. Regardless of our life or career choices, we all need an avenue for self-reflection and deliberation. While our connectivity with the world continues to increase, our yearning to consciously disconnect is greater than it ever has been.

In many ways, this whole cycling venture was about taking this principle to an extreme. One of the reasons it appealed so much was the opportunity it offered to seek places where being electronically reliant was of less importance. Perhaps that explained why I chose the left turn at that T-junction. Taking the right and following the Silk Road was the recognised route. Take the left and there appeared to be very little ahead of me. There was also total disconnect.

Time to consciously listen to music, audiobooks and podcasts; to listen to the words rather than simply hearing them. Space to think, write and reflect. I could have chosen a different route across a different country. I could have sought mountains, rivers and cities which would have provided a more diverse photographic collection. I sought the monotony of the Steppe for exactly those reasons: time and space.

**3.**

The daylight hours were getting shorter. The morning chill was notable after a night in the tent but, as my body adapted, I began to embrace the crispness. My routine had become more flexible. I rode when I wanted, stopped when it felt right and proceeded again when my body and mind said so.

Every day, my legs resented being put into motion after lying sedentary since stopping the night before. I never rode with my headphones in for the first hour of the day. Without audio distractions, I was forced to set my intentions and embrace my surroundings. I had spent the previous fourteen or so hours inactive but the physical movement and exposure to nature geared my brain into action.

I broke the day down into segments, evaluating where I was, where I might get to and where I might find supplies en route. There was usually a small, nondescript cafe somewhere along the road. It was hard to determine where and when. As usual, I just rode blind – 'hope for the best, prepare for the worst'.

I began to understand my own mentality more as the miles ticked away and the hours alone clocked up. Almost every day was mentally tasking, even the good ones. I neither resented nor celebrated how my morale changed. I sometimes wished my overthinking mind would desist but I adapted the best I could. The peaks and troughs of my emotions and thoughts when alone presented a difficulty I had not experienced before.

The final hour of riding was a highlight of my days. I was used to inclement weather including thunder, lightning and storms from time to time but I became downbeat if it turned sour in that period. I mellowed knowing that another day was behind me and I was a bit closer to my next objective. The mellowing was part of the process, of the peaks and troughs. I didn't like ending a day on a ridiculous high or low; it felt wrong. It was important to end in a mood of serenity and reflection. I needed to be able to give myself a heartfelt reminder that this was the right place to be at this time of my life and that the next day, the next week, and the next checkpoint, were worthwhile goals to work towards.

One day I stopped at a hut on the side of the road. I was near a mining site and an unexpected little hill was ahead, the first I had seen in Kazakhstan. An old man emerged. We were, as I had become accustomed to, confused by each other's presence and our inability to communicate. With my very basic Russian and his equally basic English, we tried to muddle through.

Despite my protestations, he remained convinced I was American. He went to his hut and came back with two carrots. With his left hand, he held the base of the carrots, standing them upright next to each other. Then he lifted his right hand and, making the sound of a plane as he swayed it from side to side, crashed it into the carrots, knocking them over. This was followed by both hands coming together and exploding outwards. The image was instantly recognisable. Like almost everyone else, I recall exactly where I was when the Twin Towers happened: in the second row of a geography lesson in a small, chilly temporary portacabin classroom.

I was curious as to why this old man on the Steppe had brought up the Twin Towers. I assumed he was just making a cultural reference about where he believed I was from. But then, becoming increasingly animated, he gestured towards the hill saying, 'No, no, no.' He pretended to shoot a gun into the air and motioned as if to cover up his face with a balaclava.

My mind was buzzing. The idea of terrorists here in Kazakhstan seemed an absurdity but I couldn't ignore the man, could I? Only a few months earlier in Tajikistan, there had been a coordinated ISIS attack in which a car with five men inside rammed into seven cycle tourers; the men then attacked the cyclists with knives and an axe, killing four of them. It was a savage story which constantly ran through my mind as I was riding. A random occurrence, a tragic anomaly, but still it had happened. I often thought about how I would defend myself and what I would be willing to do if I had no other choice.

In Italy, I had been in a supermarket, my bike locked up outside. As always, I had taken my handlebar bag with me –

it included my essential items, phone, passport, money and a few other things including a knife. As I left the supermarket, I saw a man trying to cut the lock on my bike. I took out my knife and ran towards him. Thankfully, he backed away. It is rare my temper flares but I suddenly felt so protective. He couldn't understand as I mouthed off at him explaining that the bike was my whole life. Still with my knife in hand, I rode away and gestured towards him. I still don't know what I would have done had he not backed away. I remain grateful I didn't have to find out.

Doing reconnaissance work in the army, we were trained to note the absence of the normal and the presence of the abnormal. The situation I now found myself in was abnormal. My knife was the only defensive weapon I had. Should I wait and listen to the old man or go on ahead along the only road? I chose the latter.

I removed my headphones and had my knife opened in my handlebar bag. I rode up the hill and could feel my heart racing: I was fearful. I got closer and two figures emerged. I rode closer still and was grateful for the clarity of my vision: balaclavas, goggles and military camouflage jackets. I stopped where I was, looked around and analysed the light brown rocky texture of the ground around me. There was nobody else, just those two. No weapons were visible. They didn't move, or get out their phones as if to coordinate others, and nor did I. I waited and worked out my next move. It might have been nothing, but I couldn't be sure.

More time went by and I knew there were only two options: either wait for a car and get a lift or use the movement of a car to enable me to pass. I was against getting a lift of any sort so I chose option two and waited.

Two cars were approaching up the hill a mile away. The bend in the road meant the two men couldn't see the cars but I could. I waited. The men didn't move. Finally, I hopped back on the bike and continued uphill slowly. They moved into the middle of the road and my heart raced. The cars were getting closer. I then slammed down the pedals hard, took out my knife and rode straight. The cars and I reached the two men at the same time; they jumped aside and we passed by. The cars sped ahead, and I briefly looked around and saw the men running.

I pedalled harder, panting madly, until they were out of sight. I slowed down and continued to ride for another few miles. I got to the top of the hill, stopped, sat down on the side of the road and ploughed through a couple of cigarettes.

I didn't know what to make of the situation. Nothing had actually happened. I was neither attacked nor harassed. It had been a non-event and yet it felt significant. I had felt, for pretty much the first time on the trip, scared for my safety. Managing fear is often a rational process – *if* you can manage the controllables. This incident, however, made me realise that should someone take an aversion to me, there was little in my armoury to enable me to do anything about it. I was alone and vulnerable on the Steppe.

Cycling in shorts, a T-shirt and a cap made the trip feel less like hardship and more like fun, despite the austere surroundings and the odd bout of unfavourable weather. I was almost trying to trick my own mind. Wearing my cap was meant to force it to understand that the trip was about freedom, about creating my own rulebook and not just spinning pedals mile after mile. I wasn't here just for the cycling; I was here for everything else.

Up until this point, I had been wearing my trusty sandals. Although they looked normal, their unique feature was their cleats on the bottom which clipped into the pedals. As someone who has spent much of their life cycling, I wholly embraced this invention. Clip-in shoes or sandals massively increase your power output. Wearing trainers, a rider only generates downward power on each revolution. With cleats you generate 360-degree power and, with thousands of miles ahead, this would make a difference. I was not racing anyone but throwing away speed for the sake of it made no sense. In addition, sandals don't stay wet when it rains, don't absorb sweat and don't smell. There is, however, one major disadvantage and it was heading my way.

As the temperatures dropped, I was still making progress, learning and thinking about my surroundings, but everything was a little harder. The roads felt stickier, the nights were longer and the mornings harder to get up for.

When in Aktobe with Yerlan, we had browsed around an outdoors shop for a suitable set of boots for winter. I needed warmth but also a degree of flexibility and manoeuvrability. I cared little about brands and more about functionality. It reminded me of when I was in a climbing shop looking for mitts for an Antarctic expedition. I had little money so was extremely conscious of the prices. I was asked a simple question by the shop owner: 'What price do you place on your fingers?' Here was a similar scenario where the wrong purchase could end in frostbite. As much as I tried to ignore what lay ahead, I couldn't deny reality.

Eventually I chose big, black, clunky, warm, Kazakh-made worker boots. Having purchased them, they sat at the bottom of my right rear pannier and I was content with them safely nestled there, despite the significant extra weight. The weather was still agreeable but unfortunately things would soon change.

I pitched my tent amongst a small clump of trees near the road. The atmosphere felt different; not freezing but bitter. I had a few days until I reached Astana but Kazakhstan had decided the time had come. I removed my pedal wrench, tried to remember which way to unscrew the pedals, and yanked upwards hard. Poor Dorothy looked unhappy without her cleated pedals, as though her sole purpose had been temporarily removed. I dug into my bag, removed the boots and my spare pedals and made the change I had been dreading. It meant a change of seasons, a change of mentality and a different kind of challenge.

It dropped to -8°C overnight and I took a photo in the morning of a frosty tent and a dusting of snow on the hard ground. I shared the photo and said, 'Winter is finally here.' An experienced cycling friend of mine responded by saying, 'That's not winter, it's the end of autumn! Brace yourself. When it's winter, you'll know.' The comment went round my head as it certainly felt wintery. Or perhaps because deep down I knew he was right and this was just an aperitif.

---

The wind was a nuisance. It never seemed to support where I was going and, even more frustratingly, I allowed it to influence my mood. I told myself again you can only control the controllables but the wind seemed unresponsive to my daily requests. More effort, less speed. I was familiar with this awkward cycling maxim. I still spun the pedals the same number of hours per day, but I travelled less far.

Every few hours I would come across a dingy bus stop – this despite never seeing a bus – and seek shelter from the elements. Ambient chill is one thing but wind chill is the real killer in extreme surroundings – it ripped through my clothing and was a reminder of my erroneous cost-cutting purchases. My comfort levels were decreasing. I knew Astana was getting closer, though, and with it would come a sense of completion.

When there were no bus stops, I paused next to drainage tunnels and sat out of the wind to mentally decompress. When riding, so much and so little happened. My mind was never truly relaxed; it bounced from one subject to another. My music stimulated thoughts about different people, places and memories. As always, there was nobody else to discuss things with.

Each stop was important. I always looked forward to these pauses, so it was irritating when a spot wasn't quite right; when I couldn't find somewhere to sit, or the wind direction was unfavourable, or there was nowhere to rest Dorothy. These inconveniences were never truly demoralising but they added up. I was usually happy chatting to locals but often, during my rest stops, found myself indifferent. Instead I took my headphones out, slumped down and processed what had gone before and what lay ahead. I needed to listen to the environment and absorb my surroundings. I didn't always need conversation; on some days, progress and introspection were enough.

I could happily sit and observe the world go by, watch the few remaining crops in the fields compliantly swaying in the breeze, or a sequence of characterful clouds drifting by. Simple observations, from the angle of the sun to the bland-ness of the colours and the texture of the soil, provided a sense of continuity which I appreciated while allowing me to gauge subtle changes in what was around me.

One afternoon I sat and a watched a bustard merrily wandering around in front of me, its presence providing a welcome moment of company. A car had pulled up and two men came running out with a square pillowcase in hand and headed straight for it. The bustard darted about, throwing the two men off course. It waited until they edged closer before abruptly reacting and bolting between them. Finally a third man came hurtling down to join in the chase. It was only then they spotted me watching them.

Thousands of miles of the Steppe lay beyond, with little variety of flora or fauna, and yet here were three Kazakh men edging ever closer to this solitary bird. They laughed and shouted each time the bustard got the better of them. As with a mouse seeing an approaching cat and relying on guile and agility to survive, size was against the bustard but decisive action, speed and surprise were in its favour. It would lull the men ever closer, stoically positioned in one spot, the pillowcase hovering menacingly in their hands. Then, as they lunged and dropped the pillowcase, it would whizz away dramatically and find another place to stand, leaving them in a cloud of dust. Only once did the bustard take to the air. And even then, it was an unnecessary final flourish to assert its dominance over its would-be captors.

The performance was a sharp reminder that the bustard, alone on the Steppe, was in its true element.

The three men joined me and we laughed as I showed them their failed chase on video. When they left, I was none the wiser as to why the bustard had appealed to them but it wasn't hard to guess. They had probably spent at least four hours driving since the last town with minimal distractions.

Catching a solitary bustard on the side of the road was something to do, a story they could tell afterwards.

Their engine started again, I pushed down on the pedals, and off we went in different directions along the tarmac strip dissecting the nothingness beyond. I would likely never see them or the bird again.

---

Kazakhstan is the ninth-largest country in the world with one of the lowest population densities. The Kazakh Steppe, covering approximately 310,600 square miles from the southern edge of the Ural Mountains to the northern shores of the Caspian and Aral seas, is the largest steppe region in the world.

The climate of the Kazakh Steppe is characterized by its distinct seasonality, determined by its location away from seas or oceans and a consistent presence of wind. Summers are typically hot and dry while winters are perishingly cold. Temperatures range between 40°C and -50°C.

The people in the small rural communities I came across led hard and simple subsistence lives. I saw cars outside their homes but rarely. The small roadside cafes – my saviours from the wind and a reliable source of sustenance – were usually located in the front half of homes. They were family-run, generally by the woman of the household (sometimes assisted by a daughter), while the men worked outside. Many of the men I encountered were truck drivers, others farmers who rarely left their land. Rural Kazakhstan was a patriarchal society with clear gender roles. The men I spoke to took pride in their stature and, the larger the belly, the prouder the man.

High-street fashion was out the window here but laughter and community spirit were not.

Often in normal life, we are so absorbed in our own worlds, routines and stresses that random acts of kindness skip us by. We believe we're too busy to partake. These small acts, however, can have the biggest impact. I was usually greeted at these cafes – in fact, across the country – with both confusion and generosity. Being a stranger in a place with nomadic traditions had extraordinary upsides and not a day went by without someone offering me something.

I remained grateful for each encounter. On every occasion, somebody took time out of their day and removed themselves from their own world in order to bring something to mine. The selflessness I met with made me re-evaluate my own life. Would I – do I – act in the same manner? Would this journey impact on my commitment towards the world and the people in it? Would it make me a better person? I hoped it would.

Beyond requests for selfies, and there were a lot of selfies, I had encounters with the most amazing array of individuals. Rarely could we convey what we wanted to say, so I would often just say the name of the next town to indicate where I was going. If the conversation extended, I would say, 'Astana', and smile as the expression on the person's face grew confused; to them the idea of riding a bike hundreds of miles to their capital was clearly ridiculous. Encountering men, and it usually was men on the roads, I was often met by a firm grasp of my legs and the widely acknowledged signs of a clenched fist and tensed bicep, followed by a rotating finger near the head and crazed eyes. 'You are very strong, but very crazy.' It became a theme as winter settled in.

Bizarre and awkward gifts received from locals stood out amongst my repetitive existence. Just as darkness was falling, but before I began my search to find somewhere to pitch my tent, I stopped at a small petrol station to grab water. It was closed but a van emerged and five men piled out. They were confused by the sight of me but, almost without hesitation, handed me a cigarette and water. This was followed, virtually automatically, without clear conversation, by a five-litre plastic bottle containing a mystery juice and two enormous foot-long Kazakh sausages. I could do nothing but smile, express my gratitude and somehow work out how to attach it all to my bike.

The juice was awkward to transport and would almost certainly freeze overnight. It felt absurd but I couldn't refuse such a gift so I bungeed it all down and pedalled away with a dinner-for-one freshly prepared.

Then there was the time when I had just left a small town and was feeling sprightly, having had a cup of tea and a few biscuits. There was a crispness in the air and blue skies all around; even the dullness of the Steppe seemed more lively. A few miles outside the town, a car pulled up ahead of me.

I debated whether I should stop or ignore it; I wasn't always in the mood for small talk or putting on a polite face for strangers. I didn't feel like chatting but I stopped by the driver's door seeing he'd already unwound his window. He handed over two slices of warm pizza, gave me a high five and drove off with a thumbs up out of his window.

He might have been full, he might not have liked the pizza, he might have been about to throw it away. But I'd rather take the act at face value and draw the conclusion that he was a good man doing a good deed. It is important to believe in humanity and the goodness of people or our worlds start to become vacuums of hope. I am not so naïve as to believe everyone in every situation does the right thing. But, if given the choice between optimism and pessimism, especially when journeying alone, you need to maintain the former to sustain a sense of purpose and hope.

---

The distance to Astana was decreasing and I could give my hosts an estimated arrival date. Sharing an aim with others is a surefire way to focus attention and increase motivation. With a clear target established, I was unable to make excuses to myself for elongated rests or late mornings. It was getting colder by the day and icy roads and falling snow were recent additions to the daily grind. I wheeled my arms around each morning to get the blood flowing to my fingers which struggled with the metal handlebars. The tyres I had were adequate for almost all conditions but their tread would be unsuitable on the icy roads in the months ahead.

The first snowfall of the year usually brings with it childish excitement. Having strong crosswinds drive snow into my eyes, however, was less like childhood fun in the Hampshire fields and more reminiscent of climbing expeditions. The sausage I'd been given froze overnight and became nothing but an effective truncheon should any person or animal act in an untoward manner. One of my full water bottles froze solid as well but, not wanting to throw it away, I had to accept a one-kilogram dead weight attached to my frame for several hundred miles. When packing up my tent, the frost that had accumulated on it increased its size, despite a few minutes spent bashing it off and losing dexterity in my fingers in the process. My phone battery was starting to decline, my sleeping mat was not thermally efficient enough and a few of my toiletries had become ineffective. Each day was a learning curve but a reasonably gentle one which gave me food for thought about what I'd need to change when things got properly serious.

Except for a collision with a swinging taxi door on my exit from Istanbul, I had been fortunate in terms of injuries and crashes. I didn't trust riding on these icy roads, though, and I know Dorothy didn't either. On the penultimate day before reaching Astana, I was tucked into the side of the road, gingerly navigating my way around patches of snow and ice, when my attention was redirected. Four empty cars were lined up on my side of the road with lights flashing. Just beyond them, men with ropes were hauling up a fifth car out of a small ditch.

Having been on the receiving end of so much kindness, I thought about stopping. And then reckoned against it. As I passed, however, I thought, 'No. You have to stop and help, they would do the same for you.'

Cue to an immediate and regrettable slamming of the brakes and a huge skid on a patch of ice. I went down with a thud. Water bottles, sausages and other random bits and bobs skidded across the temporary ice rink. I could sense all eyes had turned from assisting the car to the felled cyclist. Feeling enormously self-conscious, I sheepishly picked up my belongings, hopped back on Dorothy and pedalled off as quickly as possible without looking back. I was embarrassed. I had neither achieved my aim of assisting them nor maintained dignity by effortlessly gliding by. It also hurt. I had torn my clothes and cut my skin. I was aggrieved by my own idiocy but it could have been worse and it was something to learn from.

I sent a picture of a road sign showing the distance to Astana to my hosts, Andrew and Fiona. The capital was only a day away now, albeit a long one, and the thought of warmth ahead was enough to keep me going. There was still no visible sign of the city, however. This was not like Paris or Istanbul where the outer suburbs stretch for miles around. Even when I was apparently only an hour away, I was still in the middle of nowhere.

There was only one road, so I would get there eventually. With the target so enticingly close, though, I was tetchy about my progress and frustrated I could not move faster. My bike was beginning to make more unnerving noises. We both needed a system reset.

Then there appeared, almost like a medieval castle surrounded by a moat of water, this high-tech, high-rise, modern city surrounded by nothingness. It was indeed, as Yerlan had informed me thousands of miles before, 'an oasis in a desert'. It was Astana.

Traffic lights, exhaust fumes, expensive cars, luxury buildings, modern architecture – this was like nowhere else I had been. I pedalled past a McDonald's and a Starbucks. There were people. On the Steppe I had been reduced to fleeting encounters in tiny villages; the sudden presence of advertising hoardings, street lights and office blocks seemed out of kilter with my own understanding of the country.

I had one immediate objective, which was to take a photo in front of the ninety-one-metre Kazakh Eli monument. The height is associated with the independence of the country in 1991 and, for me, represented my arrival. I was finally in the capital of Kazakhstan.

# 4.

Having had a job in which I had a regular salary, a uniform, a photo ID card, a pension and potentially stable employment for twenty years, choosing the life of a rolling stone was the other end of the spectrum. I had no organisation looking out for my welfare and no certainty ahead. My life had moved from an army barracks where I was surrounded by friends and like-minded individuals, with regular meals and showers, to being alone, living out of a tent and grabbing food and a wash as and when I could. Everything about this life was at odds with what had gone before.

In the army, fulfilling and demanding though it was, and despite progressing at your own pace and in your own direction, there was a recognised path to follow. There was a support structure above and below. To leave, to set off on a new life, with zero structure and zero support, was liberating.

Alone on the Kazakh Steppe, I was free from timetables and rules. The expanse of physical space around me and the miniature world I had created for myself gave absolute freedom. I could wear what I wanted, stop when I wanted and sleep where I wanted. It was a selfish luxury.

Despite its perks, it came at a cost. The financial cost was minimal but the social impact had been great. Several months of intermittent small talk and a lack of real connection heightened my desire to seek the opposite. I needed a short-term sanctuary to recalibrate, and it came in Astana.

I held the buzzer down and heard a British voice telling me to come in. I needed no second invitation before rolling my snowy bike through the side gate of the two-storey house. Fiona smiled, walked down the steps and gave me a hug. I apologised for the filth on the bike tyres, the panniers and my boots. I apologised for my own smell and that of my clothes. I think I had become immune to such things during my routine of cycling and camping but arriving in someone's home made me self-conscious.

I hadn't met Andrew and Fiona before. They were acquaintances of a friend of mine with whom they'd had a chance encounter in Kyrgyzstan months earlier. I was put in touch and they had kindly agreed to host me for a short period before I continued on my way. It spoke volumes about them both that they were willing to host a fellow Brit on a bike cycling across the country.

'There's the sitting room, dining room and kitchen. There's your room, your bath, shower and towels. We're off for drinks at the Ritz Carlton soon with some friends. You're welcome to come along but, equally, feel free to stay here if you like. The taxi is coming in half an hour so it's up to you, we're totally easy either way.'

With a pannier in each hand, I ambled up the wooden staircase to my room, complete with a beautifully made-up double bed. This alone seemed an odd concept but it was not the time to overthink my fortuitous situation.

I stripped off, wrapped a towel around my naked body and pottered through to the bathroom; my own bathroom. I looked in the mirror and noticed the visible weight loss. My legs were okay but my upper body was less muscular than when I had started in the summer. My dirty feet made a mark on the pristine white bathmat, a reminder that they too hadn't been washed in a while.

I turned on the shower and the glorious flow of warm water rained down onto me. Relief. It was cleansing physically but mentally as well. I stood and tried, in those brief moments, to recap the past few months but instead little snapshots flew in and out of my mind, as they often did while riding. I was happy to just be in a shower, happy to be in a home and happy to be safe. The reflections, the internal musings about what had gone before, and what was to come after, could wait; this was not the time.

Instead, this was a time to be joyous and grateful. I dried myself off – a second, more thorough wash would have to wait – got changed, and headed down to the kitchen in slightly more civilised clothing than when I arrived.

Fiona gave me a beer and we exchanged small talk about what we were doing in the middle of this enormous country. They had moved out here with Andrew's job in the army, having previously been posted to a variety of other interesting spots around the world.

Andrew connected to the Sonos system and out came Fleetwood Mac's 'Everywhere'. While riding, I was restricted to my headphones and the internalised focus that creates so missed surrounding music in a room. I was pleased to know that, if nothing else, there would be a musical understanding between my new hosts and me.

———

The taxi arrived and, not long after, I was sitting with a group of English-speaking strangers in the lobby of the Ritz Carlton. Instead of finding a source to top up my water bottles and bread to survive on until the morning, I was sipping cold beer with smoked trout canapés. Instead of using body language to inquire where I could buy toothpaste with a local shop owner, I was discussing the Kazakh stock market and oil industry with an Australian businessman.

I had spent months on the road a little uncomfortable about the environment and culture I was riding through, but had tried to adjust; and now, oddly, I felt similar sentiments in this five-star hotel. I was in a safe setting, but I was still the odd one out, still the outsider and still being constantly questioned about who I was, where I was from and where I was going. Being alone on the road gave me an openness to unusual situations, which came from constantly expecting the unexpected. As usual, I projected an image of joviality but I still felt an emotional disconnect.

To so many people I had met in impoverished communities on the road, I was viewed with intrigue but also with a degree of sympathy. People could see I was a homeless wanderer, a vagabond. The sight of my clothes and equipment indicated I was not just out of place but also in need of assistance. Locals would go out of their way to show support at their own expense. They would do this out of the goodness of their hearts to show love to a foreign traveller in their land. They assumed I knew nobody and little. When I explained I lived in my tent and my life was just the six bags around me, there would be a look of sadness and confusion, almost pity. So many people I encountered had no comprehension of why one would choose to flee their home and live this sort of existence. It made no sense to their own understanding of home, family and community.

But this would not be my life forever, nor one that had been forced upon me, but rather something I had chosen. As with George Orwell in *Down and Out in Paris and London*, this was a conscious choice. In the late 1920s, Orwell cut ties with the safety of his home and lived a life of poverty, hoping to develop a greater understanding of and genuine empathy for the disadvantaged in society. He had little money and worked for minimal amounts to simply sustain his life.

I had saved money to fund my travels. I lived a simple life on the road to sustain myself over a prolonged period in the knowledge that I could, if necessary, stop and work to earn enough to continue riding. I found, as Orwell did, that when you are without some of the basic requirements one is accustomed to for a prolonged period, your perspective shifts.

Odd as it might sound, I felt as though being able to stay in a lovely home and sip champagne at the Ritz was almost a betrayal of my life on the road. It's natural to feel guilt and introspection when your lifestyle shifts so dramatically in the briefest of time periods. To so many people I met, my solitary, stripped-back image generated compassionate emotions and a desire to help. But those who assisted me were usually far less well-off than I was. This did not stop me accepting their generosity. On the contrary, I welcomed it. Part of me resented my own weakness in accepting their gifts, but I also understood that it came from their own goodwill.

I was told that the city was representative of the inequality and social diversity in the country. As the families who had lived in the city of Akmola, before it was renamed Astana in 1998, sustained themselves in small service industries and endured the winter through profits from their market stalls, others revelled in the new-age city built around them. Still drained from the desert, drinks at the Ritz felt as surreal as it was memorable.

---

I was often asked where my home was. The problem was, I had no real answer. Usually I deflected the question with, 'I am from the UK but currently my home is here, living on my bike.' This explained my circumstances but gave away little about my emotional state and what it felt like to be thousands of miles from friends and family. For my own sanity, I had to see my life on the road as a form of home, despite the obvious reality that by living out of my bags and sleeping in a tent, I was, in a real sense, homeless.

If home was a feeling, then staying with Andrew and Fiona in Astana gave me that. Their love for one another provided an emotional warmth I lacked. Their home was, for a time, my home. We ate, drank, watched movies, listened to music and read books. By staying with fellow Brits, Astana almost felt like a place of familiarity and comfort. Much to my gratitude, Andrew and Fiona never expressed stress or discomfort at my prolonged presence as I worked on the bureaucratic logistics for the next chapter of my journey. I hoped perhaps it was even a welcome interlude for them.

Sometimes I explored the city, wandering about in the freezing temperatures swathed in hats, gloves and scarves, tiptoeing my way around the icy streets. At other times I was largely sedentary, unmotivated to socialise despite welcoming the interactions when they came. On the road, I had only the briefest encounters where simple explanations were sufficient. Many of my internal thoughts were weighing me down but they could not be expressed with sufficient depth due to the language barrier and the time available.

Because of Andrew's job, I was invited to attend various social gatherings. A notable occasion was the remembrance service on 11 November, held at the Palace of Peace and Reconciliation, one of several Norman Foster architectural designs in the city. The international ceremony was held inside the vast stained glass and granite pyramid as the thermometer plunged to -25°C outside and my own alarm bells rang as my clothing proved useless against the ambient chill. As locals in the old town continued their daily grind, the dignitaries of the city gathered. Medals, shining regalia and prestigious artefacts adorned many of the military while others sported smart suits and slick haircuts.

I stood on the beautifully polished floor in my hefty Kazakh boots, an old black long-sleeved Under Armour shirt, a ripped down jacket and a set of multiuse outdoor trousers I had found in the market a few days before. My hair itself was less rogue than the grade two I had when I left, but it was certainly not smart. I stood out like a sore thumb.

It made me think of where I'd been the year previously, dressed up in an army uniform at a training regiment, surrounded by new recruits just starting their military careers. With a sharp haircut, pressed uniform and highly polished silver, I had blended in. Despite having only left the military a few months before, I was now an object of suspicion. Yet as soon as I said who I was staying with, why I was in Astana, what my plan was and what I had done before setting off, people were respectful and enthusiastic.

Through the unexpected nature of what I was planning, I continued to make local and international friends and was actually happy amongst this diverse crowd. I drank with some, lunched with others and had interviews with representatives of a few local news outlets who were generally confused by me but pleased with what I was doing. Each encounter taught me something new and helped me contextualise my experiences and weave together a greater comprehension of the intricacies of the country, its history and traditions. Astana represented the modern, outward-looking, progressive Kazakhstan I had heard and read about but, until now, not seen. Oddly, my journey across the Steppe provided others with insights into places they had read about but not seen either.

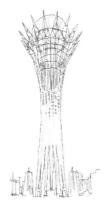

The Baiterek Tower in Astana represents modern-day Kazakhstan. According to Kazakh legend, in the desert stood the Tree of Life, a *baiterek* or poplar. This mighty tree supported the whole world with its roots reaching down into the underworld and its crown extending into the clouds above. Within the branches of the *baiterek* tree lived a mythical bird, Samruk. Nothing was more beautiful than Samruk, and, as a messenger from a higher being, only she could distinguish the sinful from the saved. Only through Samruk could the divine mystery of the world be revealed.

Each year, Samruk laid a golden egg between the two upper branches of the *baiterek* tree. The egg symbolised the sun, granting life and hope, while a dragon below, Aidakhar, wished to eat the egg. The drama repeated itself infinitely and represented the cycle of winter and summer, day and night, and the struggle between good and evil.

---

There is never a perfect way of cycling around the world in terms of seasons, certainly not when your departure date is determined by your employment status. You have to compromise on something. The problem isn't working out what the best time of year is, but rather how to avoid being in a particular place at a particular time. For some, winter in Kazakhstan is as bad as it gets. For others, it could be summer in the Australian Outback or the monsoons in India. I had made my bed in terms of departure dates and route choices; I now realised I had to sleep in it.

Astana is the second-coldest capital city in the world after Ulaanbaatar. I had become accustomed to it but only in the way the Kazakhs do: that is, by wrapping up to the maximum for the brief periods of time you are required to be outside but otherwise staying inside where it's safe and warm. The winter months in the harshest places on earth are not the time to be gallivanting outside and the minimal daylight hours only add force to the argument.

However, regardless of what everyone I met suggested, I was departing in a couple of days. I wasn't sure whether it was even possible but, by not accepting the impossibility, I had given myself a chance.

There were two unavoidable issues while I remained in Astana. First were the practical preparations. This was not just a short camping trip for a few cold sleepless nights. It was also not a self-sufficient Antarctic expedition where everything you'll need is on your sled. Being on a bike, you have to compromise and remain as adaptable as possible.

I spoke to a polar-exploring friend about travelling solo in remote cold environments. I read blogs about cyclists who had done similar things. I reread passages from books I had photographed in preparation for this exact moment. I tried to utilise all the lessons I'd learned from climbing and military expeditions but this would be unique. There would be no teammates, no sergeant major, and it wouldn't be anybody else's job to ensure my safety.

Again, I needed to adopt my old climbing mantra: 'Prepare for the worst, hope for the best.'

Due to Kazakhstan's surprisingly prestigious cycling history, I was able to scout out a bike shop I'd heard could assist me. The thirty-minute ride there itself was informative when I saw a reflection of myself in the shop window with a frozen beard and sore eyes. I looked at sleek carbon bikes with narrow tyres and enviously picked them up with a finger. I watched video clips of glorious French mountaintop finishes with sweaty riders collapsing in exhaustion at the finish. I then looked outside at the icy roads and my heavy steel bike.

I explained to the shop owner, Anatoli, what I needed and where I was going. He saw it as a joint project and together we spent a few days tweaking and rebuilding Dorothy to be capable of dealing with what was ahead. We sat and spoke about anything and everything while eating dumplings and sipping tea.

The whole process of preparing Dorothy was another example of people going out of their way to help me. I finally left with a few presents from Anatoli: a wolf alarm and two balaclavas. He believed in what I was trying to do and respected the boldness (or perhaps stupidity) of my plan. 'You are very strong, but very crazy,' he said.

On the bike, I now had an additional front rack, three thermos flasks, new studded tyres and camel-wool-wrapped handle-bars. On my person and in my panniers I had down gilets, down jackets, goggles, face masks, four buffs, several thick pairs of socks, several types of gloves, two hats, three gas canisters, an extra roll matt, an extra sleeping bag, thermal trousers and spare thermal tops. I was barely able to lift it all up. The idea of pedalling anywhere, let alone up hills or into headwinds, was beyond my comprehension.

---

Logistical hiccups are an unavoidable reality of travelling, especially in remote places. I had read books of travellers and could not grasp how they had spent hours and days waiting for visas to be processed, passports to be stamped and entry to be authorised. My own travels over the years were usually specific one-off trips. Bicycle travel is less certain. Timings are harder to predict, routes change and accommodation is transi-tory. Additionally, it is an unusual way to cross a border so alarm bells are immediately raised among those in charge. I was conscious of this but had still not experienced the wrong side of it.

My plan, despite the cold, was to depart Astana as soon as possible, head into the Kazakh part of Siberia and continue east until I entered Xinjiang in northwest China. That in itself would, I knew, raise issues. My rough aim was to then cross Mongolia to Ulaanbaatar, drop south back into China and push towards Hong Kong before winding down through Southeast Asia to Singapore. This meant a multiple-entry visa for China was necessary as well as a Mongolian one. The latter was not expected to be an issue but I knew the former would.

My timings were slipping. I appreciated the opportunity for recovery but was frustrated at having to wait for the bureaucratic process. Every day was getting colder, snow was falling and my Kazakh visa was nearing its expiry date. I was also spending money while stationary. I processed my Mongolian visa quickly at an added cost and then spent weeks trying to sort things for China. As stories from other travellers had warned, I had to queue up outside the Chinese Embassy each day and hope my persistence would get me through the door. In freezing temperatures and snow, I would diligently pack up my documents and wait. Rarely was anyone let in and more rarely still did they re-emerge with the approval they sought.

I spoke to anyone and everyone I could both in Astana and back home to try and assist in the process but there was little progress. Was it my bike? Was it my army connection? Was it my planned route through Xinjiang? I had little clue about what was holding up the process and, more importantly, whether I would be able to sort things from where I was. Trying to translate from Chinese to Russian to English was an added challenge while persuading the Kazakh authorities I was unaware that my free visa was about to expire and I didn't have anywhere else to go. In the end, I had to pay government-approved translators to oversee my signing of a form acknowledging my own incompetence in order to be granted an extension.

Not just days but weeks went by. Waiting and being unable to do anything was frustrating. Waiting and being unable to do anything but believing you could influence proceedings was a test of patience and inventiveness. As with bike repairs, nothing creates resourcefulness like necessity. I had primary, secondary and tertiary plans with contingencies for each one. I had trains and planes as potential options that involved skipping large chunks of the map and continuing on from an easier, and certainly more temperate, spot. But the latter were a last resort: I felt compelled, if possible, to continue from exactly where I was.

Each day, Andrew would return from work and ask about my progress. He and Fiona were supportive and generous without ever pressuring me to leave. Considering they had had no idea who I was a matter of weeks before, this was genuinely kind. I felt guilty about their extended hospitality but, as they were aware, it was not through my own lack of effort.

Progress was eventually forthcoming. A team effort involving trains, couriers, multiple embassies in multiple countries and a string of false hotel bookings daisy chaining across China ensured all my visas were stamped. I had spent so much time trying to sort the issue, I had almost lost track of what this actually meant. It meant I was leaving, that the comfort of this city was almost at an end and I had no choice but to prepare for what was ahead.

---

The Swedish word *resfeber* best sums up how I felt. It roughly translates as, 'the restless race of the traveller's heart before the journey begins, when anxiety and anticipation are tangled together'. It is the nervous buzz before the gun goes for a race. Everyone is waiting at the start, knowing they've put the training in; they're making small talk but they know that, very soon, the small talk will end and the hurt will begin. It is the moment in your tent at high camp with your rucksack loaded and headtorch on, about to set off into the darkness. You feel prepared, agitated and enthused, all at the same time. You've done all you can and, very soon, the time for others to help will be at an end.

You know you'll have to sort yourself out, find your own solutions, search deep within yourself for added resolve and motivate yourself to keep moving. Nobody else is going to do it for you. That knowledge, perhaps formulated from past experience, is both a great strength and a dangerous weakness. By pushing our limits beyond our initial perceptions, those ordeals also put into perspective the challenges we've faced and how we've overcome them. They also remind us of the depths we've had to go to in order to succeed. To me, *resfeber* meant deliberating upon the reserves I was going to need over the coming months. What would I deem too great a cost? When would it be not worth it? Was this even possible?

Leaving is an aspect of long-distance solo travel that most people don't think about. People focus on the whys and hows of getting from A to B, the conditions, the loneliness, the physical effort, the homesickness. But ask a solo traveller what the hardest place to leave was and it'll jog their memory into gear. It's not just the moment of departure itself; it's the anticipation, the knowledge you're leaving, the acceptance of another relationship you've left behind. I knew things would be different when I rolled out of those front gates.

My hosts and I had a charming final meal together before I headed upstairs, took a bath, laid out my kit and set an alarm for the morning. My clothes were clean, my body recovered and my mind refreshed.

My time in the capital had been important. It was my first chance since leaving home to properly stop, process and reflect.

Antoine de Saint-Exupéry wrote in *Le Petit Prince*, 'What makes the desert beautiful is that somewhere it hides a well.' Astana is an odd city in terms of its architecture, the inequality between its inhabitants and its location on the Steppe, but I had developed a fondness towards it. With thousands of solitary miles ahead, I knew I would miss it. I had needed the homeliness, comfort and security I was so kindly offered. I had needed to think and prepare for the road ahead rather than plough on like a bull in a china shop.

Together, Fiona and I carried my bike down the steps. I gave her a hug, expressed my thanks as best I could and said I reckoned it would be okay. Neither of us was convinced. She reminded me that, should I change my mind, I was welcome back. It was a genuine offer but we both knew that, as soon as I got on my saddle, I'd be gone and would have to face up to whatever was ahead of me rather than looking back. I waved goodbye and cautiously headed off on the icy roads with a fully laden bike.

There were many things I was unsure of as I gingerly rolled away. I didn't know if my bike would hold up, whether I had the right kit, how many miles I could cover per day, how I would stay fed and watered, what the roads would be like, what my escape plan was or how I would stay in contact with people. I did not know whether I could cope. A few things I was certain about: I was alone again, winter was very much here, and ahead lay a challenge I knew would test me in ways I could not anticipate.

# PART III

## ISOLATION

*Hope is that stubborn thing inside us that insists, despite all the evidence to the contrary, that something better awaits us so long as we have the courage to keep reaching, to keep working, to keep fighting.*

— Barack Obama

# 1.

I took a video on my first day out of Astana as 40-mph cross-winds drove into the side of my face. 'Ever get that feeling like you've embarked on something a bit rash?' I said to the camera. The bike felt heavy; my legs even heavier. I had not ridden properly for weeks and the routine my body had adapted to, of getting up and riding, had come to an abrupt halt.

Navigating out of the city was another challenge. My phone was being temperamental in the cold, and the falling snow and gloves added a layer of difficulty. Ease of access to a fully charged phone was something I had taken for granted. I sensed this was the first of many lessons.

I pedalled ninety miles. I was unaware of it at the time but it was the furthest I would ride in a day for several months. Psychologically, I needed to create distance. It forced me to look away from Astana to the next checkpoint, forwards not backwards.

The sun fell fast; the lack of daylight hours would become an ongoing battle. Cycling on those roads in those conditions at dusk would be lethal with trucks flying by. I pedalled on without finding even the slightest depression in the ground that might work as a camp spot. The snow continued to drive into me. A rare motorway junction appeared ahead with a bridge crossing over the road. I pulled over, wheeled my bike through the snow and placed it up against the concrete. The spot was more visible than I would have preferred, but darkness was my friend and the bridge provided a form of protection from the wind.

My boots and trousers were covered in snow. My tyres, derailleur and chain were the same. I unfurled my tent with gloves and a headtorch on and, despite the cover from the overpass, had to grapple with the wind to stop it blowing away. I grabbed the pegs and tried to ease one corner of my tent into the ground but with minimal success. The autumnal weather had brought enough rain to allow tent pegs to enter the ground without difficulty. Now it had frozen, just securing my home for the night was a complication.

I propped up my bike, removed the thermos flasks – I had barely drunk all day – and left my cap on the handlebars. I removed the five bungees holding down my bags, removed my roll matt, my old smooth-treaded tyres I was keeping for the post-winter months, and, one at a time, unclipped the six bags now attached to my bike. I brushed the snow off my panniers and threw them to the far end of the tent. I would usually have changed clothes – one of the first things I did upon stopping – but with the weather so miserable, I wanted to get inside quickly and sort myself out under shelter.

The muscle memory and subconscious knowledge of processes formed under minimal pressure allow you to do the same under duress. Repetition builds routine. Throwing myself into winter on day one would have been foolhardy and dangerous. Part of the reason I hadn't wanted to rely on other people in Europe was this phase. I needed to have a routine dialled in I could rely on. Through the thunderstorms of Romania, the heatwaves in Turkey, the muddy hills in Georgia and the winds of the Steppe, I was able to develop the knowledge and resourcefulness to manage now. When it was bitterly cold with strong winds, snow and darkness, I was grateful I had a workable routine allowing me to disregard external complications and focus on what needed to be done. Regardless, it was a tough first night.

It had just gone 5 p.m. I peeked outside and turned my torch off. Darkness was everywhere. Sunrise was not until 9 a.m. Sixteen hours in my tent lay ahead.

My gas cylinder was cold to touch and required warming inside my sleeping bags. I had fifteen packs of noodles crushed up in a bag in my front left pannier; they were always in my front left pannier. Each evening meal would be roughly two packs depending on my hunger levels. It was cheap, functional and easy but certainly not glamorous, flavoursome or enviable. Usually, upon finishing my noodles, I felt refuelled but unenthused.

One of the great simple joys in life is a shared mealtime and the ability to converse with others. Instead, I was eating a version of the same meal I had had for months and would continue to eat for months ahead. I had no phone reception and the weather did not allow me to sit outside and reflect upon life while looking up at the stars. Rather, I had the tent zipped up and was lying on my side with my headtorch illuminating a steaming pan, an unappealing gloopy mess looking up at me. It was a means to an end: an attempt to rebalance the calorific deficit from the day and provide my body with sustenance to continue to the next. Almost every meal over winter would be the same: a means to an end.

It could be seen as a depressing snapshot. And yet, there was something wonderful about it. Solo adventurers have always found themselves in curious situations eating extraordinary things. On many great adventures, days have often ended in a tent next to a stove spooning in mouthfuls of noodles. It should almost be praised for its simplicity and the splendid history behind it.

---

I woke in the early hours to find the tent being harassed by a storm and my body shivering. The thermometer had plunged overnight. After a few hours of internal dialogue, I wriggled out of my sleeping bag, ate some solid bread with chocolate spread, had a couple of spoonfuls of peanut butter and began to pack up.

Stuffing sleeping bags into a small compression sack is a certain way of getting your heart rate up and generating body warmth. One at a time, I packed up my panniers and threw them out of the porch before following on behind. My toes immediately felt uncomfortable when pressed against the tips of the boots. To undo a few of the tent clips, I needed added dexterity so removed my gloves – the cold metal reminded me not to make the same mistake again. Heat retention is essential; reheating a cold body or cold extremities is a time-consuming and energy-intensive activity. When extreme cold sets in, you cannot waste energy. Your body is doing its utmost to retain its warmth; it wants to stay warm and you need to help it out.

I slept in a thick merino base layer. This was its sole purpose. Once a base layer is saturated with sweat, its thermal efficiency is heavily reduced. With the long nights ahead, I needed to save certain items of clothing just for the time in my tent. I did not have a specialist extreme-condition down jacket or down sleeping bag. I had to make do with the reasonably priced equipment I had found in Astana. I'd had to find a compromise between warmth, comfort, safety and cost. I hoped I had made the right decisions.

Snowy footsteps in search of another camping spot

The fly sheet of my tent felt different. The overnight cold had coated the lightweight material with frost. Despite my best efforts to thrash it away, this made it harder to compact. The same applied to my groundsheet. Everything weighed more and took up more space. I had a few sips of water, packed up my bike, attached my bungees and wheeled it out the same way it had come. Using the same track was less tiring, while also minimising the potential for snow to clog up inside my boots or around the key bike components. I got back to the side of the road, kicked off the snow from my boots and pedals, put some lube on the chain, removed my heavy down jacket and was ready to go again.

The daytime temperature dropped to -18°C. It would remain below that for weeks to come. I had three checkpoints en route to the Chinese border: Pavlodar (300 miles), Semey (500 miles) and Ayagoz (700 miles). I had left Astana on Day 113 of the trip and until then had paid for only one night's accommodation, in Aktobe in western Kazakhstan. My view was that, unless I had someone to stay with, I would camp. I was fortunate to have somewhere in Semey but I reckoned that, for my own sanity and safety, I would also need a night in Ayagoz to thaw out. I would need to break my own rule. I had a pretty inflexible budget for the trip; the end goal would not be achievable otherwise. This phase, however, would need to be taken in isolation. This was an expedition within an expedition. I knew if I could get through it and arrive at the Chinese border intact, things would improve.

I thought of the old question, 'How do you eat an elephant?' The response was, 'One bite at a time.' Likewise, how do you cycle mid-winter across northern Kazakhstan? One day at a time.

Accurately predicting my distance per day in Europe, or even in Kazakhstan in autumn, had been manageable. I would constantly make time/distance/speed calculations to work out where I needed to be and when. If I had a pre-arranged meeting point with someone I calculated what distance I needed to cover to arrive on time. Looking ahead, I could roughly predict when I would be in Singapore based on my current progress and what I expected the route and conditions to be like across the remainder of Kazakhstan, China, Mongolia and Southeast Asia.

I had brainstormed with a friend about my plan. If I normally averaged between eighty-five and a hundred miles a day, I reckoned it would drop to sixty over winter. He was surprised. Perhaps I was being overly cautious? On the contrary, he reckoned it was overly ambitious, almost naïvely so.

Within a couple of days, I realised he'd been right. The studded tyres, while adding a new soundtrack to the ride as they connected with the ice or tarmac, slowed me down. My boots, which replaced the clip-in sandals, reduced my power output. Down jackets and extra panniers reduced my aerodynamic efficiency. The snow and ice on the roads minimised my rolling speed. My physical weariness reduced the riding strength I was able to maintain. The brief hours of daylight heavily limited the amount of time I could actually ride. The gruelling routine chipped away at my enthusiasm. The sleepless nights lessened my motivation to get up each morning. The brutality of the conditions outside made me take extended breaks wherever I could find shelter. The inability to play music deprived me of an extra boost when I needed it.

In isolation, each of those factors have an impact but it's dispiriting when they're compounded. Thus, instead of the sixty-plus miles I had reckoned upon, there were days I could barely cover thirty. I would get up late and be lethargic in my movements. This led to me resenting my situation; I regretted my slow starts and reacted spitefully to the unfavourable conditions. In an attempt to remain upbeat and keep the negativity at bay, I negotiated with myself that every mile I covered was another mile closer to where I needed to go. In other words, I would still be taking another small bite out of the elephant.

I was knowingly delusional about my progress. I could not decide if this was my mind playing tricks or pure pragmatism. I spent the vast majority of time in my tent. Hours went by with little to distract me: no music, books or changes of landscape. My thoughts spun round and round in a vacuum: anxiety about the conditions heightened by the discomfort and idiocy of remaining in one place. I was caught between a rock and a hard place and both involved unremitting Kazakh freezers. Life on the Steppe never gave an inch.

I learned from numerous short-term errors: the time it took for plastic water bottles to freeze; the way my top turned into a solid block of fabric when I left it out overnight; the hard loaves of bread I awoke to when I didn't stuff them down my sleeping bag; the time required to warm my gas canisters if I didn't wrap them up; the reduced battery life on my phone if I left it out uncovered. The phrase 'Every day is a learning day' came to mind.

---

I had begun the trip with a reasonable amount of outdoor experience behind me. I went into the winter phase having done a fair bit of cycle touring in cold weather. I felt I had a good level of theoretical knowledge. In practice, however, everything was different.

I read Everest books compulsively before beginning my Seven Summits journey. They made me feel connected to the mountain. They gave me an idea of what I *might* encounter if I ever had the chance to climb it. But reading about someone else's feelings of excitement when they stood beneath *Chomolungma* and gazed up thousands of metres to the top of the world paled into insignificance compared to how I felt when I was actually there and doing those things myself.

We read people's accounts of how they adapted and coped or, alternately, failed to come to terms with situations because they give us a glimpse into the brutal and unforgiving extremes of hunger, exhaustion, heat and cold that travellers often experience. Unfortunately, to truly understand, we need to step in, commit, try, learn, stumble, fall and fail. Through those experiences, through hurt and dissatisfaction, we learn to pick ourselves up, brush ourselves down and begin again. Our mistakes provide the foundation for another attempt.

Without such experiences, we would not work out a way to adapt and overcome. We resent the pain when it occurs but afterwards reflectively bask in our ability to have fought through it.

It was the same with the mistakes I made in the first few weeks of extreme winter cycling. I didn't know anyone who had done this solo before. I had to believe it was possible. I felt that, having got through the first few days, I just needed to copy and paste the formula: struggle, strain and survive day after day. I would have to acknowledge and embrace the positives, focus on the small checkpoints and allow the big goal to take care of itself.

## 2.

Another day completed: forty miles. Pathetic really, but it was something. At the end of the day I felt better than I had lying in my tent at 10 a.m., unwilling to escape my sleeping bag.

Those long nights: the shivering, the discomfort, the internal monologues, the lack of distractions, the regret about past shortcomings and anxiety about what lay ahead. I hated being captive in my tent. But I also loved it, I needed it. It was my safety blanket at the end of the day, my way of shutting out future episodes, a refuge to snuggle up in temporarily and feel a sense of pride and happiness at what I had achieved. My tent represented my temporary home; I trusted it. Unlike the cold, the roads and the wind, my tent treated me well and kept me safe and relatively cosy. It inspired my own case of Stockholm Syndrome.

A new day and the sun had risen. The loneliness and silence of another night had passed. It was another one down, another night I would not have to experience again. I could move, make progress and get closer to China and warmth. I just needed to ride. I just needed to unzip my sleeping bag and the process would begin. I just needed the motivation. The world around me was moving on. I had to take advantage of the light; I didn't have a choice. I wondered when they'd find me if I just stayed there. I unzipped my sleeping bag, felt the cold hit my torso and zipped it up again. 'Ten more minutes,' I whispered to myself.

I slept with a buff around my neck, one around each of my wrists, clad in gloves, a hat, a neck warmer and my down jacket. It was never enough. Or at least it was never enough during the dead of night when the dark silence echoed around me. It was never enough when my heart rate was low and the blood was not being pumped around my body. I spent every night periodically doing sit-ups and leg raises to get the blood moving and my core temperature up. I would be temporarily out of breath but marginally less cold: a necessary compromise.

My new inflatable air mattress wasn't working effectively. I blew it up but after a few hours of restless dozing, I found myself uncomfortable and close to the frozen ground. I spent hours trying to locate the cause of my troubles but no air bubbles surfaced when it was submerged in water and there was no audible sound. Awoken every few hours by a surge of shivering, needing more tent exercises and to re-inflate the mat, I would curse my purchase and my failure to solve the issue. Despite not having drunk much, I would need a pee. I had to undo both tent zips, shuffle to the edge of my tent and remain in my two sleeping bags as long as possible. I would then lower the sleeping bags to my knees, crouch in the porch of my tent and undo more zips on my trousers before an unsatisfying and often quite futile urinary performance. Much effort for little reward.

I wanted to message friends and family or write down my thoughts but it often wasn't possible. The battery life on my phone was temperamental and I could not expose my hands for long outside the sleeping bag or I would lose feeling. I would then immediately place them back inside the bag next to my groin, one of the warmest parts of the body. So much of the time, I would be rubbing my feet and toes together to keep those other essential extremities warm.

Slowly, 10 a.m. turned to 10.30 and then to 11. I was still lying in the same spot I had been in for eighteen hours. I berated my lethargy but still didn't move. I hated my inability to do such a simple task. All around the world, people were going to sleep, waking up and continuing their lives. And yet here I was, alone in a tent in a ditch by the side of the road, feeling miserable and unwilling to do anything about it. 'The worst decision is no decision.' I had my old Sandhurst instructor's voice in my ear and still I did nothing, paralysed by my own indecision.

Too many scenarios and too much dread about the coming day were whizzing around my head. Instead, I chose the easy option: to do nothing. By doing nothing, I was static, I was going nowhere. By doing nothing, I was failing. I had to do something.

The internal monologue was relentless. I wished I could have just got up, packed away the tent and got it done. Perhaps if I had a friend, they would have finally yielded, said something, and the process would have begun. Instead it was just my own voice, my own fragile mind telling me the same thing again and again. I was hyper-aware of the situation and knew I was delaying the inevitable. By not actually doing anything constructive, I was engaged in this process of conscious delusion. I was lying to myself again about when I was going to get up, totally aware of the fact I was going to ignore my own promises. It could not, therefore, be lying if I knew I was lying. I knew I had had this conversation with myself already. The previous day, the previous hour.

'Just get up!' My head was banging itself against every imaginable wall. Inside, there was this awful war about what I needed to do and what I was actually doing.

'GET UP!' But still, I wouldn't move. Nobody was telling me to stay and nobody was telling me to move. I wasn't in the army anymore. Life was easier when someone told you what to do. If you weren't being told, you could follow the examples of others. If you were in charge, you felt compelled to set an example to those who were unwilling to make the first move. Perhaps that was officership: to take the lead when others had no inclination to do so.

But here, alone in Siberia, there were no soldiers and no officers, no set itinerary for the day and no enemy positions to assault. There was no motivation to get up. And yet the motivation was everywhere. I was wholly motivated, rarely had I felt such a compulsion to just do something: anything. And yet, once again, nothing. The mind was willing but the body was not. Or was it the other way around: the body was willing but the mind was not. Perhaps neither was willing; both were failing in their own ways. I was losing weight but not willing or able to consume enough food to counteract it. My body was shivering again, unable to keep itself warm when I needed it to.

When the despairing reality of my situation became too overwhelming, I made a snap decision and wriggled out of my sleeping bags. I would sort as much as I could inside the tent; the real world was a step away. Most of the time I camped in the snow – it gave my tent pegs purchase, unlike the hard

Steppe – but occasionally I met with a field frozen to its core. There was nobody else around. Not even the crops were tempted to peek outside at this time of year.

---

I thought of friends of mine who were in Antarctica. It was not as cold there as where I was, but certainly cold, and thinking of their expeditions gave me strength. I've always respected great British explorers like Scott and Shackleton for their sheer stoicism and aspiration, and Norwegians like Nansen and Amundsen for their preparation and precision. I wanted to be a combination of both. Succeed and survive like the latter, be courageous and selfless like the former. What I was doing now was not comparable to what they had done a hundred years before, but I thought of modern Antarctic expeditions and how I compared.

I knew they were struggling alone in the cold. We were each in our own worlds of difficulty, each going about our odd daily existence and trying to make progress where we could. What mattered was not who had what to eat or what safety precautions they had taken; it was more that each morning we all, begrudgingly, lethargically, painfully, got up, got out of our sleeping bags, packed away our tents and moved on. I had my reasons for doing what I was doing; they had theirs. What mattered was that we had driven ourselves to get to where we were. Nobody had made us do it.

Sometimes, you just need a boost from someone else who is also struggling but manages to keep going. That someone is usually the negative conscience in your own head, the monkey on your shoulder, but it could also be a fellow adventurer several continents, oceans and almost 9,000 miles away.

Out went the front panniers first followed by the larger rear panniers. I then had the task of putting on my boots. Over the course of winter, I relocated them to different parts of my tent to try and find the warmest spot but to little avail. The laces were rigid: they required caressing to loosen them up. The same applied for the high edges of the boots around the ankles. Actually placing my feet into the boots was another foreboding task. Finally, I half put them on, got out of the tent and stamped downwards: it was another task completed. I then tried to generate enough heat to ensure that I would still have non-frostbitten toes a few hours later when I found my next camping spot.

I collapsed my tent and packed it away. Poor Dorothy would sometimes be semi-submerged in the snow so I would knock that off and give her a once-over to check everything was in reasonable working order. There was no bike shop nearby if she decided enough was enough. Every morning I wanted to apologise to her, and often did. This was not much fun for me and it wasn't what she was hoping for either. Bikes like to be ridden; they like to be tested and not found wanting. A sturdy British steel touring bike wants heavy panniers, mud, rain and dirt roads. It wants changeable conditions, new challenges and varied terrain. For Dorothy, I knew this was right on her limit. I willed her to stay healthy; I needed her to.

I needed to fuel my body as my mouth was parched and my stomach groaning. I grazed through the long nights on Kazakh chocolate. When I was thirsty I poured tiny cups of water into the lid of my thermos and added snow to double the amount of liquid. My stove was unreliable; the working temperature of the gas ranged from 35°C to -20. Most of my nights were colder so my nutrition plans had to be flexible. Sometimes I would get a hot meal – noodles, of course – but I had to be prepared for those occasions when I didn't. I had snacks with me but they were never appealing, not at 4 a.m. in -30°C. Cigarettes out the porch were something at least, just to get me through the night.

I saved the remainder of my bread until morning. The chocolate spread and peanut butter looked up at me. They knew they weren't appealing; I knew they weren't appealing. The bread was dry, cold and cracking. There was no moisture left in anything. It was hard to get any purchase with my spoon. I needed to hack at the spread with a knife and then add a dollop onto the bread. The saying goes, 'Eat breakfast like a king, lunch like a prince, and dinner like a pauper.' I was confident no king would eat frosted cold bread with chunks of chocolate spread for breakfast, but I hoped to prove the rest of the saying wrong. Regardless of the lack of glamour, it was food, it was fuel; it would give me enough strength to begin the day.

Personal hygiene went out the window. I accepted that my general demeanour, even aroma, was not going to impress anyone. My deodorant froze so it went; my wet wipes and moisturiser followed soon after. I placed toothpaste on the high-value list, especially given my awful sugar-fuelled diet, so it won a prized spot inside my sleeping bag. Even then, the exposure during the day meant its viscosity made brushing my teeth harder than normal. I did what I could. I was hardly going to be entering a fashion contest anytime soon. My facial hair, style choices and clothing cleanliness would have held me back for starters.

And then another moment regularly battling for top spot on my 'Least Favourite Aspect of Winter Cycle Touring' list. The simple act of changing tops. Off went my down jacket, gilet and cosy merino base layer. On went my cold damp base layer from the previous day. Imagine putting on a wet wetsuit and multiply that grim feeling. When it's viciously cold outside and your body is working hard, you still generate sweat, and there is nowhere to dry your damp top at the end of a day. I had only three long-sleeved base layers. Without a nearby washing machine or place to stay, one would be used to sleep in and the other two could be rotated each week.

The dread of the moment it touched my skin was worse than the reality; and the reality was miserable. Instead of a normal base layer which might fall effortlessly over my bare torso, I would have to coerce this down as the cold wet fabric clung to my skin. I would then do star jumps to get warm, aggressively whirl my arms around a few times as my hands were chilly, put on my Norwegian bobble hat and be ready to move.

The routine changed every day based on location and weather but the general gist stayed the same. I woke often in the long, lonely nights; I dozed when I could. I survived. However much I disliked getting up, I was happier once I did. Each morning I viewed having got through the night as a success, a little dopamine hit to begin the day. Another night was over, another day was here. New challenges would invariably head my way but I was closer to where I needed to be.

**3.**

A slight loss of concentration and off it went, bouncing and rolling across the vast Kazakh Steppe. If it were not such a critical item, I would have ignored it and cut my losses. Alas, when you have no actual home, you do everything you can to preserve the temporary one you do have.

The wind had turned 180 degrees overnight. I was woken by the tent violently shaking. A distinctive cracking sound was followed by a total change in the shape of my overhead protection. Several poles had snapped.

After another terrible night I was not completely focused in dismantling it. I always kept one peg in while I unclipped the poles from the main body and collapsed the frame. Now, however, I stupidly took out the final peg prematurely, a strong gust blew and off it went. Just like that, my poor tent went leaping across the flat landscape before I had the chance to grab it. Instinct took over and off I went in pursuit.

If there was one photo I wish I had from the whole trip, it would be of this moment. Dressed in a down jacket, lycra trousers, boots and a silly fur hat, I chased after my red tent as it did its very best to flee the lifestyle it had been living. Occasionally it would slow down as the wind dropped, only to speed up again as I got closer. As the chase continued, I felt like a hitchhiker when people play the game of slowing down as they pass, making you think you're about to fetch a ride; you're all set to jump in only to see them speed off with great enthusiasm, spraying dust into your panting mouth. On this occasion, nobody could see me; I had veered well off the road the previous evening. I chased for what felt like several minutes. I've always run the 400 or 800 metres at athletics competitions and felt a similar lactic burn in my legs but sadly the endpoint in this race was not the finishing straight. The endpoint would be accepting my tent was gone and would continue to bounce its way across Kazakhstan.

A lone and leafless tree stood on the Steppe. It was probably wondering where its neighbours had disappeared to and why it was still standing in this place when, quite unbelievably, it was attacked by a tent. I finally caught up, got a firm grasp, unclipped the poles from the main body and freed the tent from the tree. There was little doubt it had seen better days but at least it was alive.

In some of the harshest sections of riding, something which never failed to bring me a smile were the cafes. They were both my morale booster and my literal lifeline, the only places for hundreds of miles where I could fill up my flasks, buy food and engage with people. I never knew quite when they would appear, which made for stressful patterns of water consumption, but I developed a blind faith in their presence.

Not being a Russian speaker, identifying shop names was sometimes a challenge but I became an expert at spotting the sign for '*кафе*'. I would prop my bike against the wall, head through the outer door, pull aside the thick inner curtain and cagily look around the room. With two flasks, spare gloves, neck warmers and goggles under my arm, combined with a frosty beard, rosy cheeks and a western European complexion, I hardly blended in. Heads would turn, eyes would scan me up and down before returning to what they'd been doing, while I found a table and assessed the menu.

I would immediately try to charge my phone, dry any wet clothes and warm up; my fingers and toes were always cold. I never understood the menu but the cafe owners and my fellow diners were always spirited and helpful. They did not speak English but this wasn't a problem; they would simply point at their food and shout at the waitress to get me the same – at least I think that's what they did. It almost always ended up being *plov*. If it wasn't *plov*, then it was a direct descendant of *plov.*

I'm exaggerating slightly but during this stretch of the trip the famous Central Asian dish and I became well acquainted. A rice pilaf with meat, carrots, onions and spices, *plov* was a staple at all the cafes I visited. Over time it became a reassuring constant in my unfamiliar – and unpredictable – lifestyle.

The cafe stops were something I looked forward to. They provided slivers of hope in situations that often bordered on hopeless. I amused the owners and the other diners by my presence but their warmth gave me far more than mere physical temperature. When things are tough, especially if you're alone, you need small things to cling on to. People often bought me extra food, tea or vodka, and I was always pleasantly surprised and appreciative – though this was tested on one occasion when a man called Maxim offered me a cold, jellified meat dish known as *p'tcha*. I later learned it was the calf muscle of a cow. On a freezing winter's day, it was not quite what the doctor ordered but, so as not to offend, polite consumption was the only option.

I was still regularly halted on the road by passing drivers who were invariably perplexed by my presence. I was given food and water aplenty and, as a suitably amusing array of selfies were taken, received plenty of encouraging remarks. Through Google Translate, or some improvised English, I understood that the general theme was, again, 'You are very strong, but very crazy.'

I believe the locals thought I was genuinely mad. Their approach to winter was to minimise outdoor exposure and only venture out with maximum clothing. To them, the idea of spending all day and night in those temperatures was, quite frankly, suicidal. On more than one occasion, drivers stopped, took a selfie and gave me money. Initially I would decline the offer but their insistence that I take it and get a meal at the next cafe was so touching that I would ultimately give in. This help was invaluable: it made me feel less exposed and less alone.

Often people stopped and offered me a lift. This was a different sort of dilemma and the temptation was fierce. Nobody would ever know; I would cover more ground in less time and get to China faster. And yet I refused every time. It made little sense to refuse a lift in -30°C, with a headwind gusting, and yet I couldn't accept their offers.

For some unknown reason, I had convinced myself I had to cycle the whole way. Winter in Siberia was *the* challenging part of the trip. If I could endure this, everything else would be okay. To get a lift would be cheating; perhaps cheating nobody but myself, as those following my trip back at home would likely not have known or been bothered, but I believed in authenticity. If I got a lift for fifty miles, then why not get one for 500 miles? In my mind, the principle was the same. Either you battled and endured, or you didn't. I wouldn't criticise anyone for adopting a different approach but I gave myself certain rules and wanted to keep to them.

———

Semey, or Semipalatinsk as it was known until 2007, is located in the far northeast of the country, in the Siberian part of Kazakhstan, close to the border with Russia. As well as being the birthplace of the great Ukrainian heavyweight boxer, Wladimir Klitschko, in 1976, it gained fame for being the location of 'The Polygon' or Semipalatinsk Test Site – the primary testing venue for the Soviet Union's nuclear weapons during the Cold War.

From 1949 to 1989, the Soviet Union conducted 456 nuclear tests at the 7,000-square-mile Semipalatinsk Test Site ninety miles west of the city without considering the impact on the local people or environment. The site itself is a similar size to Wales and has become synonymous with human tragedy rather than scientific or military greatness. Almost 200,000 Kazakh villagers essentially became human guinea pigs as they were told to step outside and watch the mushroom clouds erupt nearby. Unsurprisingly, the soil, water and air quality in the region was heavily compromised, resulting in high cancer rates and a significantly reduced life expectancy. The site is a tragic example of the generally unknown and undocumented impact of the Cold War and nuclear testing.

Russia is yet to apologise for events whose malign conse-
quences are still being felt in this part of Kazakhstan.

I avoided going to the test site but headed towards Semey
itself to meet Yernar. The connection with Yernar was tenuous
but on this trip unfamiliarity had become my norm. He was
the brother of Inara, whom I had met in Astana through Matt,
whom I had met through Andrew, whom I had met through
my friend Ed. It was one link after another and, in theory, the
chain should have got weaker but, in fact, the opposite
occurred. The more distant the original connection, the odder
my arrival and the more it was welcomed. Yernar and his
mum Nadia ran a small cafe in Semey called 'Espresso'.
Unlike everywhere else I had visited in the previous few
weeks, this was a beautifully designed and warmly decorated
spot which could have slotted seamlessly into central
London.

I arrived in a buoyant mood. A few hours before, I had
stopped at a truckers' cafe and got chatting to a few drivers. I
spent a lot of time chatting to truck drivers and they often
recognised me from the road. Within a few minutes of stopping, I had been passed a bottle of vodka by a hugely over-
weight but smiling trucker. Sergei wore grubby tracksuit
bottoms, an ill-fitting T-shirt and a hoodie and had a worry-
ingly mistreated liver. He and his friends poured not just
shots of vodka but big healthy glasses of the stuff. If I didn't
down them I received a look of collective disappointment. It
was unashamed peer pressure but, as a proud Brit, I had to
give it my best and duly obliged.

Sergei had taken great pleasure in showing me around the
cab of his truck, pointing out his cooking and sleeping
arrangements and his array of porn mags. He, like most of the
truck drivers I met, enjoyed his job, the time away from his

wife and life on the road. He missed his two children but got paid reasonably well and had regular employment throughout the year. It had been a shame to part with him but I did so rather merrier than I had arrived. Having seen the amount of vodka Sergei put away, and realising he was driving again that afternoon, made me slightly alarmed at the state of other road users.

As soon as I got to Espresso, Yernar and his mum cooked me food and made me a perfect cappuccino. I was dirty and tired but safe. It was not the glamorous or charming first impression I would usually try to provide but, given the circumstances, neither I nor they were remotely bothered.

My first night in Semey was special. From road workers and truck drivers, to shop owners and businessmen, I shared many meals with many folks on my journey, but that night was the perfect example of what the great English writer A. A. Gill wrote in his autobiography *Pour Me*: 'To feed someone is… to offer warmth and comfort, well-being and hospitality.' That night I experienced family, acceptance, community and cultural significance all rolled into one.

It was Yernar's niece's first birthday: an intimate family occasion, but I was welcomed along and treated exquisitely. Four generations congregated in one room. There was a dazzling array of traditional Kazakh food including *beshbarmak*, *shashlik*, or skewered meat cubes, sausages of horse-rib meat known as *kazy*, and *pelmeni*, which are minced meat dumplings. That was the main course; for desert we feasted on *baursaki*, which is a sweet, puffy pastry fried golden brown. We made speeches, and bestowed blessings on each other and on the baby, Diana. We drank and sang songs and they wished me good health, strength and safety for the remainder of my journey. Family matters enormously in Kazakhstan, as does kindness to strangers and those in need. It had a significant impact on me.

I remained for a couple of nights before moving on. It had taken a few weeks to get there from Astana and I still had ten days or so of riding until I reached the Chinese border. I had convinced myself that east, or more particularly southeast, would be warmer. I refused to research the matter extensively as my myth might have been shattered. I had to keep believing things would improve or I might not have wished to continue.

I parted ways from Yernar and Nadia with a heavy heart and a sore head – the last night had escalated rather more quickly than we'd planned with a few friends of Yernar's dropping by. Yernar and Nadia had sacrificed their own comfort and routine in order to give me a home for a short period, and it said a lot about them. They invited me to stay longer if I needed to but I had to keep on keeping on. The longer I stayed, the harder it would be to move. I was sufficiently refuelled and rested to make the final push to the border. I knew how much discomfort lay ahead but back to the saddle and frozen wasteland it was for the final part of Kazakhstan.

**4.**

I was restless, shivering and wishing the minutes would turn into hours and the hours would give way to the morning light. But time seemed to stand still, trapping me in an unhappy world of darkness and self-reflection. I knew I was close to the end, close to a major checkpoint and my first border crossing in months. But still the wind and the icy temperatures did not let up; Kazakhstan would not yield.

I thought about Eckhart Tolle's book *The Power of Now*. In it he writes, 'If there is truly nothing you can do to change your here and now, and you can't remove yourself from the situation, then accept your here and now totally by dropping all inner resistance.'

Tolle continues to explain the idea of surrendering to where you are, accepting it and viewing that acceptance as a strength not a weakness. To deny the reality is what creates the unhappy self, the resentful and miserable person.

I believed strongly I had to accept where I was, however uncomfortable, and not complain. I could not let myself become a victim of my own decisions. I had made the choice to be here; this was my doing. This partially led to self-doubt but it also gave me nobody else to blame. It forced me to acknowledge the reasons for what I was doing and to try and live in the present. Too much time spent contemplating the coming weeks, and the amount of resulting discomfort, would be demoralising.

The Finnish concept of *sisu*, a combination of inner courage, determination and resilience, inspired the title of my Seven Summits book, not just because *sisu* is required to climb big mountains; but, even more so, telling the story I did in the book required *sisu*. Deciding to set off on my bike required *sisu*. They were mental rather than physical battles to overcome. They were about tackling emotional doubt and social stigmas attached to what we should be doing at a certain age and the projection of a certain image of normality. Having the courage to embark on a project, irrespective of the negativity around you, is difficult and scary. Ultimately, turning inaction into progress is the most fulfilling path.

Winter in Kazakhstan certainly required *sisu*. Every day turned into a mini battle. The small things I ignored and gritted my teeth through were starting to frustrate me. I was grateful for not having a working odometer – the numbers would have made grim reading – but the cold managed to break the clock as well. I had issues fixing things. Cable ties and gaffer tape were usually the go-to solutions but, in those temperatures, the tape lost its adhesive qualities and the cable ties snapped upon fastening. I had only one puncture but it was a significant hassle. Generating the heat to warm the glue and patches required a stove. This required a warm gas bottle which, in itself, required heat. Catch 22. It took a lot of time in a bus stop and some very chilly fingers but I finally fixed the problem.

I missed my music but my headphones failed to function in the cold. I began the day with my phone and headphones deep within my jacket to keep them warm. I would then select a specific set of songs and, with my phone within a glove within a warm sock within my handlebar bag, I would have musical accompaniment for a short fifteen minutes – enough for about four or five songs – and then nothing. I removed my headphones from my ears and tucked them away again. They had served their purpose for the day.

I had to carefully select the songs. However much different music would flick in and out of my head through the day, the ones I chose for the initial stint remained with me. Would it be something motivational, emotional, melancholic, upbeat or soothing? It changed every day depending on my mood. Sometimes it was Kanye West, Muse, Shania Twain, Beethoven or T Rex. One song was omnipresent: 'Ghosts That We Knew' by Mumford & Sons. I chose it when I rode in the morning and when I arrived safely in the evening. I chose it when I was alone in my tent at night. It made me cry; it still does. Regardless of the original intention of the lyrics, they resonated with me.

That song is about hope. Getting through winter was about hope. Whenever something bad happened, I forced myself to keep going. What keeps you going every hour of every day is not just a masochistic desire to see if you can survive. I needed things to cling onto.

My hopes were for many things I was lacking at that time. It was a potential life back home with a wife and children. It was laughter with my family. It was a muddy dog walk in the countryside. It was a Sunday morning with the newspapers and fresh coffee. It was home. It all gave me hope and a reason to keep moving.

I thought about long-term hopes but what also dragged me through those tougher moments were the glimpses of pure beauty. A benefit of not having headphones was the total immersion in the world around me. It was that glorious final hour as the sun was setting and the wind occasionally dropped that revealed the extraordinary lack of noise in the vastness. It was the sun's rays glistening on the pristine and untouched landscape. It looked empty; it certainly felt empty. I would sometimes stop, wrap up warm and simply observe. I felt momentary serenity, temporary calm amidst the chaos. If I couldn't find beauty where I was, then what was I doing?

The nights also provided some of the most powerful memories. Without phone reception, social media or anybody else around, I had the opportunity to just *be*. Before the serious chill of night-time hit but after the sun had set, I could sit outside and watch the stars emerge. It was a shared sky and a shared beauty with those I loved back at home, a form of connectivity despite the thousands of miles between us. I remained in awe of the stars' magnificence and grateful for their guidance. Like the waxing moon, they gave me chinks of light and a glimmer of faith about what lay ahead as well as filling me with wonder at the world around me.

At times I felt pathetically ineffective and my life was reduced to basic survival. It was just about getting through. The tragic story of the British sailor Donald Crowhurst crossed my mind. Crowhurst's tale began in October 1968 when he set off in the *Sunday Times* Golden Globe Race, a competition to be the first person to sail nonstop single-handedly around the world. He lacked adequate funding or preparation, leaving his thirty-five-foot boat unreliable and leaky. Mid-Atlantic Ocean, he secretly abandoned the race while reporting false positions, in an attempt to appear to complete a circumnavigation without actually doing so. On 10 July 1969, Crowhurst's trimaran, *Teignmouth Electron*, was found floating off the coast of the Azores, some 1,500 miles from England. Placed in plain view were detailed logbooks outlining forged coordinates, a logbook outlining his true coordinates as well as a 25,000-word manifesto written to humankind on attaining transcendence.

After analysis of the logbooks, it was determined that the boat had been abandoned nine days prior to its discovery. The ambitious amateur had been unable to properly acknowledge the perils of his own situation until it was too late. He had forced himself into a corner from which he believed there was no escape. He had sought to prove something to someone, perhaps himself, about what he was capable of achieving and tragedy unfolded.

I was not sure what I had to prove to anyone with regards to extreme undertakings but I felt I had never truly been tested on my own. I had never felt genuinely isolated. The reality is whatever target you set yourself, there will probably be someone, somewhere, trying to better it. There will be someone trying to do it younger, older, colder, faster or further. I was aware I was not doing this for anybody else.

I once made the mistake of using a weather app to compare the temperature between where I was in Siberia and where my family was in the UK. I then thought about myself shivering in my tent alone while they were under a duvet with central heating close to their loved ones. I deleted the app immediately and concluded nothing positive could come from those comparisons.

Boosts to morale, however, came from faces both new and familiar. A car stopped in front of me near Ayagoz, a few hundred miles south of Semey. Penny, whom I had met in Astana, was conscious of my safety and followed my trip from the moment I left the capital. One of her plans was to visit the eagle hunters near the Kazakh border with China, which would take her along my route as alternative roads were somewhat limited. I was unsure when or where our paths would cross but seeing her and having a hug in this bleak setting was wonderful. I squeezed the contents of her little care package, which included chocolate coins, into my bulging panniers. She left with the line, 'You've gone further east in winter than Hitler and Napoleon did, so well done for that.'

A few days later, I had a fortunate encounter with Karin-Marijke and Coen, a Dutch couple who had been overlanding the world in their vintage Toyota Land Cruiser since 2003. When their car pulled up alongside me, I was somewhat taken aback to be asked in English whether I was okay. We pulled over and chatted roadside before agreeing to meet an hour down the road. We then spent the night exchanging travel anecdotes, ambitions, motivations and our thoughts on different countries. Again, it was a small encounter but an important connection that gave me a lift before I continued on alone.

Due to its central location, the Kazakh Steppe does not experience the same amount of heavy snowfall as mountainous or coastal regions. However, occasional snowy sections made setting up camp unnecessarily challenging. Unable to push my bike through the heavy snow, I had to make several journeys: the first one to recce the potential site and create a track, the second to take the front three panniers, the third with the rear three panniers and the fourth with the bike itself over my shoulder. I then had to flatten the surface to lay down my ground sheet before finally erecting my tent and preparing for the night ahead.

One night a few days away from China is etched into my memory. There were no trees nearby and minimal surface snow. I found a small ground depression to erect my tent. The night dragged on and on. I couldn't sleep, my teeth were chattering, my feet numb: my sit ups and leg raises appeared ineffective.

I had seen wolves from afar while riding and they are a potential threat in this part of the country. Their echoing howls often filled the void of the silence at night but I had never seen them up close. I had so many contingency plans for if and when I was attacked but theory is always different to practice. As always, I slept with my wolf alarm, headtorch and knife next to me. The alarm, I'd learned from the briefest of tests, was viciously loud but there was virtually nobody nearby who could assist even if it sounded. Would wolves even attack? Would they be scared off? Could I fight off one wolf? What about several of them? I had no idea.

Finally, 2 a.m. came around. The wind had died and was replaced by silence. I was uncomfortable but unperturbed. And then I heard a rustling sound nearby. My senses went on high alert. Silently I moved my knife to my right hand, my headtorch and wolf alarm in the other. My fear was temporarily suppressed as dealing with the current situation took precedence. I didn't know what it was out there or how big. It was still moving around outside; circling me perhaps, scoping out the situation. There was heavy breathing. Something was waiting. The calm before the storm.

So many scenarios were running through my head about what I could do. Should I wait in my tent and use it as a barrier? Should I get dressed and head out to face it? A wolf's vision at night would be better than mine but what if a light was shining directly at it? Was it part of a pack? Should I escape by bike or run? I had my pedal wrench with me as well if I needed another weapon.

As quietly as possible I unzipped the inner tent. The time had come. I was shivering. Nerves or temperature? Probably both.

One, two, three…

I yanked up the outer zip, shone my torch towards the noise and held my knife aloft, expecting to see gnashing teeth and grey fur.

Within the cone of my torch's beam, however, was not a snarling wolf. Instead, a whimpering little puppy looked back at me pathetically. The poor thing had confused eyes, was shivering uncontrollably and breathing with difficulty.

The puppy headed towards me and, dropping my knife and alarm, I gave it a cuddle, then let it lie between the inner and outer parts of my tent. My cycling trousers, previously rolled up and acting as part of my pillow, were now used as the puppy's sheet and my spare jacket was wrapped around it. I tried to offer it plain bread but it clearly lacked any sort of appetite. I didn't know what else to do.

I lay my head back down and tried to sleep. The puppy was a matter of centimetres from my face. It was wheezing with every breath and sounded painfully ill. Both of us shivering, both of us finding the strangest solace in the other's presence; a kindred soul in this inhospitable land. I begrudged the disruption to my sleep but, for the first time that winter, felt conscious that something was in greater distress than I was. It was a pathetic image: two strangers hoping to drag themselves through to the next day.

I must have drifted off sometime before sunrise. I peeled open my eyes and sunlight was shining onto my tent. But there was no noise, no wheezing, no panting. Was it a dream? I looked to my side and saw my trousers rolled out but nothing on them. The porch of my tent was slightly ajar. I raised the zip and peered around. I saw my jacket about three metres away with bit of golden fur peeking out from the edges. No movement. No sound. I crawled over and removed the jacket. The puppy's chest was motionless and her eyes were closed. It had been one night too many. I just sat on the frozen ground and tears rolled down my cheeks.

I didn't know the puppy's name, nor its owner, history or destination. In my heart, I had known when I lay next to it the night before that its days were numbered; animals in that condition don't survive winter on the Steppe. I had tried to care for it but it was beyond help. It died underneath my jacket on the harsh frozen ground. Its pain and distress were over; I was grateful for that. The vulnerable eyes that had looked back at me when I shone my torch the night before were laid to rest.

The ground was too hard and too unforgiving to dig a grave. I covered her fragile body with shrubs and said a silent prayer. I am not religious but felt as though she had found me for a reason. Maybe she had stumbled upon my tent to find a glimpse of warmth before she resigned herself to her fate. Maybe she had made her presence known to give me a sense of companionship and civility as I struggled to find either. Up until that point in winter, I had not really expressed much emotion but had simply battled on. I now briefly surrendered to sadness, having forged the most unlikely of bonds.

With only a few days left in Kazakhstan, I had to move on. I rolled up my tent, packed up my panniers and prepared to take to the road. This surreal life in this most bizarre setting was consistently filled with difficulties and emotions; loss and escape. The puppy remained with me emotionally. That small helpless creature had been sent to sleep beside me. She had been sent to give me hope in the darkness so I could see the light again the following morning.

# 5.

Since arriving in Kazakhstan from the Caspian Sea, I had seen and experienced only flat land. There had been the odd undulation but the elevation had never dropped more than 132 metres below sea level and rarely risen 200 metres above it. There are few places in the world like it. As I got closer to the Chinese border, genuine gradient changes emerged: the Altai Mountains. They represented the border and the end of my Kazakh adventure. Seeing that range was seeing the final page of this chapter of my journey. I was getting there.

I had slowly adjusted to winter cycling on dodgy Kazakh roads. Instead of snow trucks, grit or de-icer, dirt was used to counteract the snowfall. This hardly led to smooth riding as mounds of soil soon turned into blocks of ice which made each stretch of road a mini-minefield waiting to topple an unsuspecting cyclist. It's fair to say northeast Kazakhstan in winter and cycling do not go hand-in-hand. I finally turned off the potholed main road heading south and took a left turn for my final hundred miles in the country. With no attempts to make this subsidiary road accessible, despite the fact it led to the border, the track was an ice rink with a six-inch layer of fresh snow on top. It made for particularly treacherous conditions as the snow clogged my tyres, thus negating the impact of the metal studs.

Cars were few and far between, even by Kazakh standards. My frustrations got the better of me on several occasions as I slid off the track, landing with a painful thud on either my hip or elbow. Progress was slow but, mile by gruelling mile, the border town of Makanchi edged closer. I was unable to find an ATM or money exchange in this drabbest of places, only a local shop to buy biscuits and receive a vague set of directions about where I might be able to stay for the night. Through some interpretive movements, a young guy on a quadbike, under directions from his mother, led me down another snowy track – he seemed oblivious to the difficulties of cycling on snow – to a small wooden hut with trucks outside.

There was a cafe inside with a typical group of male truckers. When they realised I could not understand a word being spoken, a glass of vodka was offered instead. Eight Kazakh truck drivers and one British cyclist merrily continued the theme well into the night, cushioning the alcohol with several nondescript Kazakh meat dishes cooked by the owner. Knowing I was crossing into China the following morning should have been a reason to hold back but, once again, the uniqueness of the situation seemed too amusing to ignore. I finally rolled onto my wooden plank bed to the accompaniment of heavy snoring from the majority of those present.

I left the cafe in the morning rather worse for wear. After several months crossing Kazakhstan, I was excited to finally be making positive progress. I was cautious of where I was heading in China, aware that the region I was bound for –

Xinjiang – was a contentious one. A few months previously, I had been speaking to a fellow long-distance cycling friend, Bec, who had briefly visited Xinjiang and the situation sounded bleak. She and a friend had endured regular police checkpoints and difficult nights camping under the motorway, but she said the rest of China was worth the effort. The theme of Bec motivating me onwards was a regular occurrence. More than most, she understood what I was doing and where I was going. Her messages continued to be vital parts of the psychological armour I wore.

Kazakhstan had tested so much of my character and knowledge as a traveller, person and cyclist. Irrespective of the off-roading and time of year, just a glance at a map made the idea of ploughing through that vast country seem absurd.

Robert Frost wrote,

Two roads diverged in a wood, and I –
I took the one less traveled by,
And that has made all the difference.

I had made my choice. I had made the choice to take a road less travelled when I gave my mum a hug and left home. I had made the choice to take a road less travelled when I headed north at the T-junction at Beyneu. I'm confident that a fulfilling, difficult and beautiful experience would have greeted me if I had opted for the Silk Road and Uzbekistan but it wasn't what I'd wanted. I had wanted the logistical issues, isolation, exposure and vulnerability of looking at a map and seeing a little dot in a location where no other cyclists were. It had felt like adventure.

*Finding reason to celebrate in the Kazakh winter*

Other than the ominous calls of two crows shuffling around on the snow, all was silent. I took a video:

> *I'm in no man's land between Kazakhstan and China right now. I can't quite explain but there's a very eerie feeling. It's not helped by the crappy road, the snow or the mist. Maybe it's the region I'm going to in China or maybe it's my own nervous anticipation about what's to come. We shall see.*

Shortly after I took the video, a car came towards me from the Chinese border. I copied the video into a separate folder, put my phone away, and slowly wheeled my bike forward. The police car edged past me, did an awkward U-turn on the snowy road and followed a few yards behind.

Imposing red wrought-iron gates lay ahead of me and a pair of dragon statues were visible just beyond. Another police car was blocking the road in front. I headed right towards the border security. It was time to enter Xinjiang.

My last photo at home before departing

Heading through Eastern Europe

One side of cycling touring life: enabling daily progress

And another: enjoying the freedom of the road

Beyond the solitude and reflection, I experienced
kindness and generosity from truck drivers, road
workers and drivers across Kazakhstan

Cycle, eat, sleep, repeat:
a simple life alone on the Kazakh Steppe

Clockwise:
Arriving in Astana in October
Battling winter in Northern Kazakhstan
Wild camping in Siberia
'Subsurface life' in Xinjiang

Pedalling fast through the Gobi Desert
having made it out of Xinjiang

Changing my boots for sandals:
the moment I had been waiting for after a long winter

Different aspects of life in China: a country which
kept me curious from beginning to end

Being cheered up the final climb in
Vietnam as I approached the Laos border

Another wonderful
Warmshowers host in Thailand

Twin Towers, Kuala Lumpur

Embracing life on a beach in Thailand having
ridden from the most inland city in the world

THE SOUTHERNMOST
POINT OF
CONTINENTAL ASIA

Made it!

# PART IV

---

# LONELINESS

*What a wee little part of a person's life are his acts and his words! His real life is led in his head, and is known to none but himself.*

— MARK TWAIN

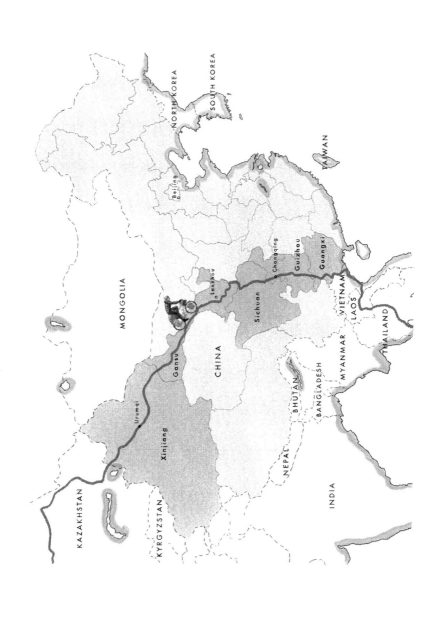

# 1.

'Always have your passport with you in Xinjiang. It is policy.'

'Always have your cellphone with you in Xinjiang. It is policy.'

'You look perturbed by the process. Please don't be nervous, we have lots of regulations here in Xinjiang. It is policy.'

Just getting into China was a logistical nightmare. On arrival, my passport was confiscated, my phone and laptop all but dismantled.

It was tiresome being told to unload and unpack all my bags, only to have to pack and load them again. It took up time and energy but perhaps that was the point. Nobody once offered to help. I was finally released from border security and taken to another holding room next to a car park while my bike was propped up outside. One person came in after an hour, gave me a cigarette and left without a word. I remained waiting, seated on a cheap plastic chair, for another few hours. No book, phone, laptop or music. I just sat and pondered my situation. I had been warned but this was more than I anticipated.

It was getting dark outside. I reckoned cycling away and finding a spot to camp might prove tricky, but I remained hopeful so long as I was released. It was not to be. I never saw the same person twice. I was escorted outside and told to put my bike in the boot of a car. I asked to be allowed to cycle but was met by a shake of the head and a curt gesture pointing out where my bike needed to go. I wedged my bike and panniers in the boot and hopped in the passenger seat.

The driver and I chatted away using a translator on his phone – I still had no means of communication. We spoke about girl-friends, families, the fear of settling down and the freedom of travelling alone by bike. We both agreed that across the world, regardless of what governments do, people have the same basic needs, fears and hopes. Chinese music was playing on a CD in the car. Bizarrely, one of the tracks was by an American country musician, Dan Fogelberg. Everything about it seemed at odds with that environment. Not only the instruments and the genre but also because the song was about freedom, individualism and exploration. My smile made him smile. I asked his name and received a shake of the head in response.

I was driven to a hotel in the border town of Tacheng. I resented having to pay for accommodation but this was not the time to argue. The policeman negotiated a lower fee for the room, £20 instead of £30, not that the receptionist seemed to have a choice. It was the most expensive place I had stayed on the trip but I appreciated the shower. I last had a proper roof over my head in Semey a few weeks before, so needed a night to charge my electronics and clean my body. I knew my clothes smelled but they would have to wait. I was told to remain in the hotel and leave my bike outside.

Having been kept in a room all day, I wanted to stretch my legs and get some fresh air, so headed downstairs. Within a minute, the driver was alongside me. Either he had been waiting around the corner or the receptionist had informed him. It was a swift response either way. He then left again and I went for a half-hour stroll to stretch my legs and satisfy my curiosity. Throughout the town, on every street corner, red-and-blue flashing lights from steel-grated police shelters indicated a near constant police presence. Meanwhile my brain struggled to adjust to the change in people's physical appearance and the language on shop fronts. My passport was requested three times by uniformed police officers.

I went back to my room and wrote in my diary:

> *I am torn already about how I approach this place. Maybe it will be okay. Maybe it is just the government not the people here. Do I see the positive in terms of individuals or do I see the negative in terms of my moral querying about what is happening? Are they mutually exclusive? It was the individuals who questioned me at the border and showed little empathy. They went through all the photos on my laptop and phone. But did they have a choice?*

I met with the same driver in the morning. Our conversation – via his phone, of course – went as follows:

'So you're in the police then?'

'No, I help the police out when they need me.'

'So you are unmarked police then?'

'Perhaps, but I can't say that.'

I was able to build a good enough rapport with him to garner a better understanding of the region. If I asked a question that went too far, the response was always, 'Sorry, I don't understand.' We were each as cagey as the other: he trying to suss out what I was doing there and I trying to suss out what was going on around me.

I knew Xinjiang was a flagship region for China's trillion-dollar Belt and Road Initiative, Beijing's ambitious programme to connect Asia with Africa and Europe via land and maritime networks along six corridors with the aim of improving regional integration, increasing trade and stimulating economic growth. I was also aware of the persecution of the Muslim Uighur population. The subject had been covered in snippets by international media outlets which I had researched before arriving.

I knew the Uighurs were the reason for the immense surveillance in the region. When Xinjiang was incorporated into the People's Republic of China in 1949, the Uighur, a Turkic people, comprised roughly 80 per cent of its population. Subsequent controlled migration of Han Chinese had reduced this share, by the year 2010, to 45 per cent. The Uighurs regard Xinjiang as theirs because they have lived there for thousands of years. The Han Chinese, however, consider it to be theirs because they have built their modern economy in its deserts and mountains.

Inevitably, there has been tension. And worse. The bloody inter-ethnic violence in the capital, Urumqi, in 2009 sent the government's repressive tendencies into overdrive. These gradually ramped up. And then, with the appointment of a new Party Secretary in Xinjiang – Chen Quanguo, a Communist Party enforcer previously in Tibet – the provincial government vastly increased the money and effort it put into controlling the activities, and the beliefs, of the Uighur population. The so-called 'Regulation on De-extremification' was adopted in March 2017. It was, said Beijing, an attempt to stabilise the region and necessary to quell Islamism.

You don't even have to live in Xinjiang to suffer from the effects of the oppression. I had met Yuan, a 55-year-old Uighur mother of three, outside the Chinese Embassy in Astana. In 2012, she and her family tried to leave western Xinjiang, where they had lived for generations, due to the instability in the region. Her passport was confiscated at the border by officials, who seized her and separated her from her family. She has not seen them since, despite numerous attempts at re-entry.

I found Yuan's story shocking but she told me it was not an uncommon one for anyone who had spoken out against the regime or tried to flee.

As part of their move to 'stabilise the region', the Chinese government introduced 'vocational education and training centres' to rehabilitate the Muslim population by way of forced integration on subjects such as culture, language and 'political awareness'. Yuan suspected her family were now living in such a centre. She couldn't know for sure and she would probably never find out. None of her acquaintances in Xinjiang could risk being seen seeking information. It is estimated, however, that the total internment numbers are around 1.5 million people. Adrian Zenz, a lecturer in social research methods at the European School of Culture and Theology in Germany, who helped expose the camps, has said there is virtually no Uighur family without one or more members in such detention. Very little intelligence is allowed to filter out. 'Massive internment camps shrouded in secrecy' is how the UN described them when it called for the immediate release of people in the camps in August 2018.

---

After a brief, ten-mile car journey with my plain-clothed policeman, we reached a set of motorway barriers, the car stopped and my bike was unloaded. A photo was taken of the policeman and me – with me holding my passport – and then he hopped back in his car. Three more policemen, also in plain clothes, then loaded my bike in the boot of their car, took my passport and we all squeezed in. Fifteen miles later, we pulled up at a motorway barrier, the car stopped and my bike was unloaded. A photo was taken of us – with me holding my passport – before they hopped back in their car and I was palmed off to another group who took control of my passport.

I was transported around by four different cars and four different groups of people. I still had no control of my passport and no means of communication. I asked each group where I could buy a SIM card but my question fell upon deaf ears. I was annoyed at being unable to cycle. I had made such a point of not hitchhiking or getting lifts on the trip, yet here I was being forced to do exactly that.

I was driven to another hotel and forced to stay there at a price determined by the police, which was non-negotiable. I was conscious of the superfluous spending. Another evening stroll was interrupted by the police. I was told I would be collected at 9 a.m. I was tempted to hit the road around sunrise on two wheels but, with no passport, I had to stay.

At 5 a.m., there was a knock on my hotel door. It was dark outside. I was still half asleep and opened the door in my boxers.

'Hello, Mr Stewart, we are from Chinese Internal Affairs. Can we talk to you downstairs in ten minutes?'

This was not a question. In Xinjiang, it was never a question.

Three people stood outside my door: two stern-looking, besuited middle-aged men and a younger woman in a navy blue skirt and blouse. The young woman asked the question – the men remained motionless and expressionless, simply staring at, almost through, me in my disordered state. She had softer features than the two men and spoke in impeccable English with a deftness of intonation in her voice. There was a disarming kindness about the way she looked, her presence and demeanour at odds with the situation. And yet she was, like everyone I had been questioned by thus far, part of the system. I obediently accepted their invitation.

'Sure. I'll see you down there.'

I brushed my teeth, threw on some clothes, grabbed my paperwork and headed downstairs to the hotel lobby where I was redirected to a small conference room in which the three people were waiting. A cup of tea and a cigarette were thrust in my direction. All three then turned their attention to me.

In her impeccable English, the young woman said, 'This is very normal, we just want to welcome all foreigners to our country and hope they are okay.'

Everyone has their own parameters of normality and, for me, this was outside my realms of the norm. I had known this part of the trip would throw up complications. But I hadn't anticipated quite the level of harassment.

'Mr Stewart, what brings you to Xinjiang?'

'I'm trying to cycle around the world. I have spent the past few months in Kazakhstan and I crossed into China the other day. I plan to cycle across the country and into Vietnam.'

Various bits of paperwork, passport stamps and visas were checked and verified. Much to my dismay, the logistical conversation went back and forth.

I assumed my backstory was already known by the authorities. I had taken the view when applying for my visa that it was better to be honest than to get caught lying – other than the false hotel bookings required for the initial visa.

Questions about my upbringing, family, employment, education and travel history came one after the other. The amount of money in my bank account was queried. I was asked where I was staying in China. Questions about my reasons for cycling led to questions about the job I had done in the army. Why I had studied history and theology at university was followed by whether I was interested in Chinese history and culture.

'Of course, your country has a long and proud cultural history I would love to understand.'

'Yes. What about the history and culture of Uighurs? Is this why you have come to Xinjiang?'

'Sorry, who is Uighur?'

I wanted to allay further suspicion. It worked: they dropped the line of questioning and moved on. Several times I asked them whether I could get a local SIM card, call my family, cycle out of here and change some money. The response was always the same: 'Sorry, I do not understand.' It was the end of the discussion.

The number of people opposite me went from three to one to five and then back to the original three. The interview lasted several hours and left me tired, hungry and irritated. I was told a car would come to collect me in an hour. Not having a passport was disconcerting: without it, I was powerless.

A car arrived exactly an hour later. I removed my panniers, removed my front wheel and loaded everything in the boot. I had seen this script before. We drove for half an hour then switched to a different car. Each time, the same process of passport photos and personnel changes. For some reason, we then veered off the main road, having been given the okay by a vehicle waiting at a junction, and headed away from my intended direction of travel. I had already realised how little input I had in our proceedings so just sat quietly deep in thought.

We drove through steep valleys and onto a plateau. The car stopped and it was suggested I take photos. Having spent thousands of miles on the Steppe, the mere presence of severe gradient changes in the form of the Altai Mountains was amazing. Snowy mountaintops jutted upwards into blue skies as far as my eyes could see. I was begrudgingly grateful towards the police officers – this time uniformed ones – for bringing me here. It might have been to show off the beauty of China. It might have been to take me to an especially remote part of the region for a different reason. It might simply have been two kind men proudly showing a tourist their homeland. Whatever the actual reasons, I said, '*Xièxiè*,' which is the Chinese way of saying 'thank you'. Finally, we all got back in the car and continued to drive around.

As day turned to night, we pulled up in another town and I was delivered to another police station. My bike was left outside the building and I was ushered inside to speak to the senior commissioning officer. Tea was delivered by an assistant and a packet of cigarettes was placed in front of me.

'So, what brings you to Xinjiang?'

'I'm just travelling the world on my bike and China was next after Kazakhstan,' I replied. I was comfortable with the honesty of my own narrative. I assumed all my information had already been passed on, though in reality, each district might have been ignorant of what I was doing.

'What do you know about Uighurs?'

When asked this question, and a version of it was usually asked, I had to tread carefully. Of course, I knew about what was happening in the region, or at least what had been reported in the Western media, but I could not say so for fear of being evicted.

In fact, I was appalled by what I had read about the treatment of the Uighurs in Xinjiang. Everything about it seemed a total violation of basic human rights, of people's freedoms of religion, expression and speech. Many of those sentiments were formed by my own background in Britain but, in my view, it is also how everyone would want to be treated: with dignity, fairness and equality irrespective of gender, race or religion.

'Why have I been transported around by the police since I arrived and why are there so many police in the region?' When I had built a connection with someone and displayed suitable ignorance about what was happening, I would ask these sorts of questions.

'A lot of police in border towns is normal, is it not?' was the response.

'Well, yes, but I have never seen anything like it was in Tacheng.'

'Perhaps not. But there is also very little crime in Tacheng.'

The responses were rarely informative but still they gave me an insight into the mindset and rationale behind what I could see. I was always being transported by the police 'for your own safety'. I had to stay in certain hotels 'to ensure the guests in our country are given the safest and most comfortable stay possible'.

From the start, I had asked every member of the police I had met about a SIM card and the opportunity to speak to my parents. The request always fell on deaf ears. My parents knew I was entering China but had not heard from me since. There was no great need to speak to them other than to allay their concern but I also requested a SIM card for the simple reason I did not like the idea they were denying me the chance to have one. The denial of outside communication is, historically, a typical sign there is something you do not want disclosed. I had been warned of this by Kazakhs I'd met in Astana, as well as by Yuan and a number of fellow cyclists who had travelled to the southern part of Xinjiang.

The border crossing and route I had chosen, especially in winter, made me an abnormality. If not directly raising suspicion, it definitely increased intrigue. Throw in my height, facial hair and complexion and you had a combination which set the alert levels to amber, likely edging towards red. I still had to be careful. If I said or asked too much then I could feasibly have had my bike confiscated, been taken to jail or kicked out the country. None were choices I particularly craved: caution was necessary.

Another involuntary night in a hotel and a reduced fee from £30 to £20: it was not breaking the bank but it was an amount I could have stretched to several days, potentially a week, in this part of the world. It frustrated me but, again, I was hardly flush with alternatives.

In the morning, at the arranged time of 8 a.m., I was transported back to the senior commissioning officer's office. Under his supervision, I removed the Kazakh SIM card, which was then confiscated, and replaced it with a Chinese one placed on the desk. Not for the first time, my phone and passport were then taken away. I was provided with another throat-scratching cigarette and left alone.

My phone and passport were then returned and the senior commissioning officer shook my hand and wished me a pleasant stay in Xinjiang. I was returned to the hotel in an unmarked police car and then left alone. For whatever reason – the distance from the Kazakh border, sufficient questioning, the realisation I was not a threat or sufficient device tracking – that was it. It left me as confused as when I began. I put on my gloves, buffs and windproof jacket – the temperature was still hovering at -25°C – and gently walked Dorothy away from the hotel. I hopped on the cold hard leather saddle and pedalled away from another place I had no intention of visiting again.

I had over a thousand Xinjiang miles ahead of me. For now, at least, it looked as though instead of being in the back seat of a four-wheeled vehicle, I would be back on the two wheels I had become accustomed to.

**2.**

Surveillance in Xinjiang is total. If it's not the police that follow you, it's the cameras, software and fingerprint scanners. It was revealed in February 2019 that a Chinese facial recognition company, SenseNets, has been tracking over 2.5 million people across 6.7 million location points daily.

As I cycled, I would reach a different police checkpoint every fifteen to twenty miles. Some 30 per cent were simply motorway barriers. As each day went by and I became increasingly frustrated, I simply rode around the barriers, keeping my headphones in and my eyes facing forward, and ignored the commotion that invariably took place behind me.

At least 50 per cent, however, were formal checkpoints. These involved parking my bike, having my fingerprints, passport and face scanned, potentially an interview or two with policemen and then having my phone analysed. Having to hand over my phone began to annoy me. My photos were dissected and arbitrarily deleted; not just the Xinjiang photos but ones from my past as well. I had backups but the very idea seemed inappropriate.

The final 20 per cent of checkpoints were especially time-consuming. They involved the same process as the formal ones with individual scans but, in addition, required all my kit to go through the equivalent of an airport security scanner. At least once a day, I would have to unpack, transport, scan and repack all my kit. Because it was winter and because I had an enormous amount with me, this procedure irked me. I was conscious of items being confiscated: gas bottles were at constant risk. I had taped my knife to the base of my saddle – a recommendation from other cyclists to keep it out of the eyes of the police. These checks usually included an extended 'tea-and-cigarette' interview about what I was doing in Xinjiang, where I stayed, how I funded it, where I had been and where I was going. All were familiar questions that I grew tired of answering again and again.

Then there were the non-checkpoint checkpoints. These were continual yet unpredictable. I would be pedalling away on the hard shoulder and then either flashing lights would emerge in front of me or a car would simply stop. Both were a clear hint I should do the same. On the few occasions I pedalled past, feigning ignorance, the result was a significantly displeased individual behind the wheel. The process, as expected, involved a quick chat, a photo of me with my passport and a gentle enquiry as to where I was going and where I was staying.

---

Pedalling through towns became games of cat and mouse. I also had to become very selective about what time of day I passed through: once bitten, twice shy.

One evening at dusk, approaching a town, I reckoned I would grab a quick bite to eat, fill up my flasks and then pedal on and find somewhere to camp. I passed police stations on both sides of the road as I entered the town but rode on. I then passed another pair of stations and took the same approach. I thought I'd get to the edge of town before finding a small cafe. It was not to be. A police car emerged ahead of me and another behind. I stopped and was told to turn around and head back to the station.

More tea, more questions. It had happened so many times yet still irked me. Even worse, it was dark outside and I had yet to eat after a day on the bike. I left the station with my front and rear lights on, planning to get food and keep riding. I soon realised a police car was following ten metres behind. I rode out of town and it remained. I rode a bit faster, then a bit slower, painfully slow at times, but still the car maintained its distance. I stopped for some food. The car stopped ten metres behind me. I stopped for a pee. The car stopped ten metres behind me.

Gradually 8 p.m. turned to 10 p.m. Then it got later. I rarely rode at night and was increasingly agitated by the presence of the car. Finally I stopped, rode back to the car and spoke my mind. Thankfully, the policeman spoke no English or I would probably have ended up in serious trouble, though the gist of my rant was probably clear. I then typed out a message on his translator app – my Chinese SIM card did not allow Google – enquiring why he was following me, what he wanted and how long he planned to continue. I said I didn't like it, I was fine without him and could he please leave me alone.

He responded by saying that he had been told to follow me to check I was okay and he was just trying to keep me safe. He then offered me a conciliatory smoke which I accepted. Afterwards, he turned around and, I assumed, returned to the town. I continued for another few miles, found a ditch on the side of the road, put up my tent and slept until sunrise.

―――――――

Shortly after being given my SIM card by the police, I removed it, snapped it in two and threw it away. I carefully scanned my phone, restored the original settings and deleted several apps that had been installed.

It took me a number of attempts to locate a new SIM from small phone shops but eventually I made progress when I got chatting to a couple of young male shop assistants. With a bit of gesticulating and the use of a translating app on one of their phones, I managed to explain what I needed. A few questions followed and I walked away rather more pleased than with the SIM given to me by the police.

Each afternoon with my new SIM, I received a text message with a weather forecast. Considering my Internet access was often limited, this was of genuine practical assistance. Each text would begin with my vague location, followed by the broad overnight weather, temperature range and wind. This was followed by the same information for the following day. For example:

> Shihezi, day to night, cloudy, -20 to -25 degrees, no continuous wind direction, breeze. Tomorrow day to night, cloudy to cloudy to sunny, -22 to -27 degrees, west wind, 3–4 level breeze.

There was a clear usefulness here but the real gem came in the second part of the text: the daily advice. Directly quoting China Mobile Weather, a few of my personal favourites were:

The winter solstice to the cold, the cold, is the coldest season, to add clothes in time, pay attention to cold and warm.

The weather is cold, and the shrimp contains protein, carbohydrates etc. It has the functions of nourishing yin and strengthening the spleen and smoothing the blood.

Weather cold, can wear a knee to do a knee warm warm to prevent the cold warm to induce arthritis.

If there is a small area of skin damage or burns or burns, apply a little toothpaste to stop bleeding and relive pain immediately.

The appeal lay partly in the message they were trying to convey but also in the translations. I was amused by the idea of reliving, rather than relieving, my pain having applied toothpaste to a small area of skin damage. Consulting China Mobile Weather was part of my routine which raised a smile at times when I often lacked a sense of humour.

---

The distrust and scrutiny were immense. Even after I'd been allowed on my way, I was under constant watch.

After wild camping for so long, I had developed an instinctive sense about where a suitable spot might be and when the best time would be to move. In Xinjiang, the police demanded to know where I was staying every night. Taking advantage of their ignorance about cycling speed and logistics and my own troubles with Chinese pronunciation, I could give them an idea of where I had come from and where I was going even if it was unrealistic. I would not tell them I planned to camp or I would have swiftly ended up in the back of one of their vehicles again and found myself driven to a hotel. I hated being tracked.

Movement was severely restricted. I was only allowed to cycle on the hard shoulder of certain motorways; they all had barbed wire on either side despite thousands of miles of desert lying beyond. If there was a snowy trail to escape down, I would veer off in search of freedom. On such occasions, it was never long before I heard the horn of a police van behind me. I would be asked for my passport and escorted back to where I could be watched.

The only available option was to camp underneath motorway bridges. Sometimes in sizeable concrete structures, other times in shallow drainage ditches only as wide as my tent and as high as my chest. These places were usually dark, dusty, cold and layered with rubbish. The time of year meant snow and ice had built up by the entrance of the tunnels. The concrete was unforgiving and establishing a stable tent position was a continually tricky problem.

A key skill in army reconnaissance is establishing subsurface observations posts, OPs for short, which enable concealment, access and observation of a particular person or location. What I named 'Subsurface Life' in Xinjiang did little for my morale but it was discreet and it was also the only choice I had to exercise a limited amount of freedom.

It was about this time that I lost access to the Internet and the VPNs I needed to leap China's great firewall. I couldn't even make phone calls. At this point in the journey, instead of the usual barbed wire lining the motorway, there were vast stretches of ten-foot-high wall. I was passing one of the 'vocational training centres' the authorities were so obscure about, which could house up to 1,200 people.

Only a few months before, China's state broadcaster, CCTV, had featured a fifteen-minute profile of life here. The impression given was of a summer camp, with balloons in the cafeteria and students playing table tennis, folk dancing and learning skills such as hairdressing and carpentry.

'It is not mistreatment,' said Li Xiaojun, the director for publicity at the Bureau of Human Rights Affairs of the State Council Information Office. 'If you do not say it's the best way, maybe it's the necessary way to deal with Islamic or religious extremism, because the West has failed in doing so… Look at Belgium, look at Paris, look at some other European countries. You have failed.'

Meanwhile Deputy Foreign Minister Zhang Hanhui was paraphrased as saying, 'Xinjiang's counter-terrorism and de-extremism efforts have created a new way to solve the symptoms and root cause of the difficult global issue of counter-terrorism, and are worthy of praise.'

Neither mentioned the political indoctrination and abuse former detainees have talked about. Neither mentioned that Muslim names were no longer allowed to be given to children, that the Uighur language was vanishing from schools or that dancing after prayers and specific Uighur wedding ceremonies and funeral rites were prohibited. Neither mentioned that minarets had been largely removed from all the mosques, and if identified entering a mosque, state employees could lose their jobs; retirees could lose pensions and owners of independent businesses could be sent away for political indoctrination and training. All seemed complicit in the enforcement of an information blackout about the crackdown. Pedalling away in the sub-zero cold, I knew a very different story from the official one that was playing out behind those walls.

My enthusiasm for where I was, not to mention my own cleanliness and sanity, was declining daily. The cold was physically sapping my energy and the fitful sleeps were adding to a general sense of lethargy. Each night under a bridge, each snapped tent peg, each interaction with the police, wore me down. As time went on, I became less tolerant and less forgiving.

On Christmas Eve, I navigated my way into the 3.5-million-person city of Urumqi, the capital of Xinjiang and the most inland city in the world. I was feeling melancholic but knew that, at Christmas, I needed to find some semblance of humanity. Arriving at night in the snow in this enormous city was difficult. One approved hostel had been mentioned to me and thankfully a spare bed was available in a shared room.

I looked and felt grim. It had been weeks since my last clothes wash. It had been equally long since I'd experienced a pleasant interaction with someone in English that wasn't a form of questioning. I chained up my bike, put my clothes into the wash and, after a shower, crawled under the duvet.

I woke in the morning to the sound of three men gently singing the Christmas carol, 'Silent Night'. The men were from Cameroon and were in Urumqi working as translators. The two other residents of my room were a Pakistani businessman and a Japanese cabinet maker. The Cameroonian gentlemen had been in the hostel for several months while the other two a few weeks.

They each said 'Happy Christmas' to me. Everything about it felt surreal. I had gone to bed in an empty room in a total haze of exhaustion and woken up to carols and an extraordinary selection of people. Arguably, it was exactly what you should expect in a hostel in Xinjiang.

I wandered into the city in a daze, uncertain about where I was and what sort of culture I was in. Up until then, I had only experienced the desert and small towns; this was quite different. I could still not make sense of the shop signs while the sheer size of the multistorey buildings, with traffic whizzing frantically below them, left me anxious and confused. I was grateful to be able to walk about and not be stopped by the police but was overawed by everything else.

There was obviously no sign of celebrations anywhere but in my headphones I had Christmas carols playing. It was absurd but I clung on to my sense of Britishness and cultural pride because I was so lost where I was. I tried not to think too much about it.

I also had a very specific mission, which was to find a new tent. The poles on mine had become unmanageable, testing my resourcefulness to its absolute limits. Metal clamps, rods and tape had temporarily done the job, but it needed replacing. It had survived some truly horrendous weather and, even after the poles had snapped, had stayed well enough together to last me to Urumqi. But a new home was on the agenda and, for just £40, a new home was eventually found.

I bought food and gloves from street sellers, laughed at a small statue of the beagle Gromit, from the animation series *Wallace and Gromit*, decorated with a Union Jack, and grabbed a couple of cans of beer. I was not in the right headspace for lengthy tours around the city.

Despite having spent so much time by myself, I wanted to be alone. I needed mental space to be able to write about Xinjiang thus far. I needed to understand what was happening and why. I needed to share it with other people but knew I couldn't. This story would have to wait until I was out of China but it was cathartic simply writing about it.

---

A proud moment of acceptance in the cycle-touring community had taken place in Astana when I was invited to the 'Cycle the World Q&A' WhatsApp group, having been sent the link by Bec, the fellow tourer from New Zealand. The group was for riders from all over the world on a range of weird and wonderful trips. Discussions were often logistical: visas, routes, borders, SIM cards, hostels, safety. They were sometimes social: riders would meet up through the group if they knew they were close. There was also plenty of practical and humorous advice about bike-related incidents and damages. Together, we had seen or experienced most mechanical issues possible on a bike so could come up with temporary or long-term solutions when problems emerged.

My favourite day being part of the group, bar none, was that Christmas in Xinjiang. It started when a guy sent a photo of himself in a Santa hat with a local family in Cambodia; someone had seen him alone and invited him to join their family. What followed was a continual flurry of messages from people in all corners of the globe, from Alaska to Ushuaia, Sydney to London, Addis Ababa to Xinjiang. Some in shorts and T-shirts, others in down jackets and woolly hats. Some were group photos with friends, family or strangers. Some were selfies in a tent or from above the clouds in the high mountains.

I was in a part of the world where I knew nobody and felt horribly lonely. Sharing those messages with so many people I didn't know, and likely would never get to know, gave me a sense of community and solidarity I had not foreseen. It made me smile because I felt I was not alone. I knew there were others like me on their own adventures for their own reasons, away from their family and friends, who also would have valued those pictures. I will forever be grateful for the strength and morale the group gave me when I needed it most.

That Christmas will remain with me also for the immense support I got from my friends. So far in Xinjiang, I had posted a lot less on social media than at other stages of the trip for practical reasons, but at Christmas I had Wi-Fi in the hostel and was overwhelmed. I appreciated receiving messages from so many people whom I would not have expected to hear from. These were small gestures on a day when the senders were likely busy with their own families but took the time to reach out to me in China. It meant a lot.

Speaking to my family meant even more. I missed them enormously, especially at Christmas. I was happy they were together, happy I could speak to them but was sad not to be in their presence. As I had found when I was climbing, especially on the two birthdays I'd spent at the base of Everest and a Christmas in Antarctica, these big expeditions are inherently selfish endeavours. There are clear upsides but they come at a significant cost. This awareness made me question my rationale for what I was doing.

Before leaving Urumqi, I made a number of tweaks to my bike. Dorothy had battled through tough winter conditions for many weeks and, within reason, had held firm. A notable plus side to riding through China, as opposed to Kazakhstan, was the road quality. It might not seem a major factor but having total confidence in the tarmac in front of you brings with it the benefit of speed and also mental relaxation. The tarmac in China was impeccable.

When it snowed, the road was cleared immediately; de-icing trucks ensured that all main roads were always accessible. As this was the case, I decided to ditch the studded snow tyres and revert to my old ones I had carried with me. To change them was a hassle but it gave me a mental boost, almost tricking my mind into thinking that I was going to a better place where normal service could be resumed.

Typically, my first day out of Urumqi brought heavy snow which made for an anxious and cautious hour but soon I was back on the road, riding faster and grateful to be rid of the constant soundtrack of studs against tarmac. I was stopped at five police checkpoints.

It was the same story for the next few days: quicker cycling, constant checkpoints and living under bridges. I was counting down the miles and the days to escape. Everything was going to be different once I had left Xinjiang. The rest of China was going to be warmer and more accessible; I just needed to keep going. I continued to be riled when the police detained me for unnecessarily long periods but mainly because of the impact on my momentum. I didn't like it but I didn't have a choice.

Each afternoon, the sun would begin its journey towards invisibility, at which point I would ride for another thirty minutes or so before finding a suitable tunnel for the night. The idea of anyone camping under a bridge was too absurd for any driver to suspect but I would nonetheless wait until no cars were visible before hauling my bike down the steep gravel section below the road, then gently lower it to tunnel level and settle in.

Sometimes I had phone reception, but most of the time I didn't. There were pros and cons to both. On 30 December I received a message from a friend when I had just nestled into my sleeping bag. My morale was reasonable and I was glad to be safe for the night. The message read: 'Safe riding, you're living the dream out there. I for one am seriously jealous, many of us wish we could do what you're doing. Happy New Year if we don't speak tomorrow.'

I was both appreciative of and saddened by my friend's message. He didn't use social media so knew little about the specifics of my trip. If he had, he would have seen that the dream I was living was sleeping in a frozen drainage ditch in northwest China. If he knew how I had felt for the past month, he would not have viewed it as any sort of dream. I would not have wished my past month on anyone, friend or foe.

It is one of the dangers of these grand adventures: perception versus reality. I tried to convey the reality to people rather than just the glorious views and romantic sunsets. The reality in Xinjiang could not have been further from the perceived beauty of cycle touring. Informative, fascinating, shocking, confronting – yes, it was certainly all these things. But if it was a dream I was living, it was sadly a warped and far from pleasurable one.

On New Year's Eve, as had happened several times before, my SIM card was cut off. No Internet, no WhatsApp, no communication, no explanation.

The day before, I had received a message informing me that a close friend had been murdered in the most savage of circumstances. It shook me up enormously. Everything about the situation was shocking both because of what had happened and the emotional connection I had with her. I felt so many things but immense anger and sadness were closest to the surface. The situation and chain of events that had occurred would enter my mind again and again throughout the ride. Everything about it felt abhorrent when I thought of the wonder and beauty of the person. The words 'unfair' and 'tragedy' do not even come close to describing it. I searched for answers but found none. For her family and closest friends, her loss must have been beyond comprehension.

In light of this, I lost my composure at a police checkpoint when they deleted photos clearly not related to Xinjiang from years earlier. They then wanted to search my bags. I was so disillusioned by the process, I swore at them and walked off, pointing at my bags indicating they were welcome to inspect them if they wished. I stood nearby to calm down. If it wasn't my boiling point, it was pretty damn close. They struggled to understand the pannier clips and the bike was too heavy for them to move it inside. Eventually they glanced notionally in the two rear panniers and let me go.

Usually I enjoy meeting people, engaging with them, understanding what makes them tick and what matters to them in life. I did not like this side of my character coming to the surface: a resentful and embittered aspect I had not experienced before. In turn, I was disappointed with myself for not coping better; for not showing more humility, politeness and respect.

I'd had an idea of what to expect in Xinjiang before I arrived and had wanted to maintain a level of dignity throughout. I'd failed. Everything about what had happened to my friend and where I was had got the better of me.

The sun was setting. I found a drainage tunnel, erected my tent and settled into my sleeping bag. I dozed and listened to music as the minutes ticked by. Finally 23.59 turned to 00.00 and 2018 turned to 2019.

I lay there and felt pitiful about this self-imposed isolation and self-imposed loneliness. Without the Internet, I had no means of messaging anyone. I missed my family and my friends. I wondered what they were doing right now and how they were celebrating the turning of the year. I thought about where I'd been the year before and how things had changed. I thought about where I might be this time next year.

I thought a lot about the inconceivable murder of my friend. I was, I am, hopeful about individuals and the goodness of humanity. I am also realistic enough to know this is not present in everyone. But knowing someone closely who had found themselves on the wrong end of what I would call evil – this was something I had never considered. The more I thought about it, the more despondent I became. And yet I had been treated so well by strangers for so much of the trip. I just felt deep confusion and even deeper sadness.

In some ways I was grateful not to have Internet access. It stopped me looking up my friends on social media and seeing how they were spending the day. It also stopped me putting on a front and posting light-hearted or jovial messages utterly disconnected from the frustrated longing I felt. Social media had become an avenue to express how I wanted to feel rather than how I actually felt. I put on a melancholic playlist and cried. It was the loneliest I had felt the whole trip, for years, perhaps ever. I had refrained from showing those kinds of emotions to anyone at home and certainly to the authorities here. Finally I was able to truly accept how I felt.

Two days later, when my phone came back online, I received a text from China Mobile Weather:

> Shihezi, day to night, cloudy -23 to -16 degrees, no continuous wind direction, breeze; tomorrow day to night, sunny -22 to -15 degrees, no sustained wind direction, breeze. New Year's Day is here, I hope all the troubles will come to an end, and the bright future is now open!

This left me as baffled as all the other messages I had received from China Mobile Weather. I hoped they were right. I very much hoped the troubles – my troubles, the troubles of the Uighurs in this shocking place – would come to an end.

The misery and tears of New Year's Eve were necessary. I had needed the emotional outpouring I had been subconsciously restraining. My mood marginally improved as the number of days before leaving Xinjiang grew less and less.

**3.**

Being in Xinjiang had taught me a lot. It made me realise I never wanted to be somewhere like it again. I wanted to work hard in the future to help ensure our democracy is maintained, our basic civil liberties are furthered and we continue to allow freedom of speech, social tolerance and religious expression. It is not naïve to believe in a society which treats people with dignity, kindness and respect, as opposed to suppression and hostility. I will continue to believe in those principles. Without them, our society will have failed.

I had not been imprisoned or suppressed or had my passport permanently confiscated. Nor had I been separated permanently from my family. I felt oddly grateful to have experienced the treatment I did, as it enhanced my awareness of the ongoing situation. I pedalled past empty villages which had evidently been cleared within a matter of weeks. I spoke to Uighur shop owners who were terrified by the thought that they, or their families, might be arrested at any moment.

I am a British traveller who simply passed through Xinjiang. I cannot claim to be an expert. However, the harassment I received from the police, the vulnerability I felt at the hands of the authorities and the clear restrictions put upon me in terms of movement, communication and speech, are things that will remain with me. If nothing else, I am grateful for the experience because it taught me exactly what I want to avoid in my own country.

―――――――

One of the basic joys of cycle touring, in fact of any kind of cycling, is the feeling of freedom. There is the simple pleasure of being outside, alone or in a group, and of having the opportunity to go where you want according to your own timetable. If you feel tired, hungry or cold, you adjust accordingly. If you want to go fast or slow, you do so. But the principle is the same: you are at liberty to choose what you do.

Long-distance cycle tourers, especially solo ones, take it to an extreme. They – we – are freedom seekers. Perhaps not forever, but for a period of time, we want to push boundaries. While alone on my ride, I tried to accept my solitariness and embrace this genuine 'once-in-a-lifetime' opportunity because, respectable and enviable though that solo freedom might be, it is not sustainable for normal life and can't be found everywhere you visit. It can't, for example, be found in Xinjiang.

Five miles before the border with Gansu province, I stopped at a rock formation on the side of the road. I wheeled my bike to it, put on a warm jacket, climbed to the top and sat down. For over an hour, I sat looking back over Xinjiang and into Gansu beyond.

I had received a message from Penny in Astana earlier that day. It read:

Xinjiang. What a place. No doubt hugely frustrating for a weary cyclist, but to witness Orwellian practice first hand is a rare insight. Like a war zone, a warped privilege to experience.

I contemplated the point of these experiences we put ourselves through: the hardship, instability and isolation. Maybe it was a kind of warped privilege to experience, as Penny suggested – a perverted desire to consciously seek wrong in order to give you an understanding of right.

As I approached my final police check in Xinjiang, barbed wire continued to line the sides of the motorway. Either side of the checkpoint, I could see it extending into the desert. The policeman and I shared a civil conversation in broken English; he wished me good luck and gave a wave as we parted ways. I looked ahead and the barbed wire was no more.

'Hope for the best, prepare for the worst.' As always, I hoped for something new and exciting ahead. If nothing else, I was confident the difficulties to come would not exceed the challenges of the previous month.

In front of me still lay snow-covered desert landscapes and a quiet motorway; that had not changed. But I had crossed a border. I was now in a new part of mainland China.

## 4.

I rode hard and fast after the border: fifty miles the first day and eighty the next in order to arrive at a town and check into a hotel for two nights at a total cost of £15. Luxury. Admittedly, my concept of luxury had been somewhat warped, so simply seeing a mattress and a shower now felt luxurious.

I ate. I drank. I spoke to my family. I wrote. I rested.

It's impossibly hard to compare individual experiences during my trip. Whole stretches of road, hundreds of hours of new experiences every day in Europe, the Kazakh Steppe or the Gobi Desert are condensed into single sentences. Some particular moments are hard to recount but at the time matter immensely. The first sip of cool water in a hot desert when your throat is raw and your water bottles are empty. Eating a meal when ravenous, showering for the first time or crawling under a duvet having slept in your tent for weeks. The moment you cross an international border, escape a particular region, summit a gruelling mountain pass or whizz down the other side. It could be a phone call with a friend, a particular sunset, a lake or a cool beer. Some occasions are euphoric while others derive their appeal from a sense of satisfaction and relief.

I had to cancel Mongolia from my itinerary. I had a visa and the country was high on my list of places to visit but not this time. I knew it would be even colder and more remote than Kazakhstan. I justified my decision by saying that the risks were too high, and potentially they were, but in reality the very thought was too much. Together, Siberia and Xinjiang had broken a part of my exploratory optimism and I felt I had suffered enough; I wasn't ready to hit those depths again. Everyone has their limits and, after the previous few months, I had found mine.

By land area, China is the second-largest country on earth behind Russia. I now plotted routes across the country on a variety of maps with the aim of reaching Vietnam. I would now go from Gansu to Sichuan, Guizhou, Guangxi and then into Southeast Asia.

A sign, the first one I had seen with English subtitles, read: 'Dry Barren Desert Nature Reserve'. Desert cycling, as I had experienced in Kazakhstan, has its pros and cons. The wind was an inconvenience but the tarmac was quick and smooth. I returned to my desert routine and short days meant I was efficient in my movement making briefer stops and riding with purpose. I was grateful not to have headphones shutting down from the cold and my choice of music changed to represent my mood – angry and melancholic tunes replaced by upbeat and optimistic ones. I was especially grateful not to have my progress halted every hour by the police. I spent the first few days anxiously waiting for a tap on the shoulder or a car to pull up alongside me but, to my ongoing delight, nothing materialised. This was neither a tourist spot nor was it a police-patrolled region.

My bike was still in the heavyweight division but, like a boxer preparing for a big fight, I was trying to shift the pounds to move faster. I was obsessed about progress to warmer climates. A glance at a satellite image showed I was in a browny-beige section for another 1,000 miles before I would encounter greenery, rivers and mountains. I missed rainfall, flowers and colourful leaves, simple boosters to one's mental state.

Navigation was hardly an issue; I remained on Route 312. There were enough small towns and cities along the way that basic logistics didn't prove too troublesome. Without the barbed wire, I could easily pull off the road and find somewhere to pitch a tent; the barren Gobi Desert had its advantages, however unwelcoming it might have been.

I spoke to a few great friends when I found a camping spot in the evenings. My SIM card, although restricted by the Chinese firewall, which denied access to Google, WhatsApp, Facebook and Instagram, was able to keep me connected to people through a virtual private network or VPN.

I began to listen to podcasts and read again. The sheer strain of life over winter and in Xinjiang, even disregarding the logistics, had made any sort of cerebral concentration hard to manage. My brain had begun to narrow so much to the essential tasks of staying alive and making it through each day, I had given up on intellectual stimulation. But now, the landscape of the Gobi allowed my mind to wander and face the reality of my own thoughts. I needed the desert, and the positive energy it provided, even at such an austere and unforgiving time of year.

China is a country of 1.4 billion people – a truly staggering statistic. Its presence on the global stage is undeniably huge. For context, the GDP of China in 2019 was $14.14 trillion; the US GDP in the same year was $21.44 trillion while the UK was sixth on the list with $2.83 trillion. China has experienced exponential growth over the past few decades. With its closed, centrally planned economy it has, through manufacturing and technology, become known as the 'world's factory'. It is the number-one export country in the world.

Through work and expeditions, I have travelled a lot, and actively seek to develop my knowledge of the places I visit with an open mind, aware that my perspective is shaped largely by my upbringing. Travel shifts our own concept of normality as we directly experience and witness other people's normal. China had already stretched my mind and I knew it would continue to do so. I wanted to learn and absorb what I could. I knew my experiences in Tibet on my Everest expeditions, and more recently in Xinjiang, were far from representative of the whole country. I needed to suppress the negative sentiments I had and replace them with a willingness to discover the beauty of the country.

Moving on from the deserts, the scenery and culture began to change. High mountains reared up and steep valleys became the norm. I spent each day ascending long, winding mountain passes and flying down the other side. I was eager to push towards Vietnam but each day took longer and required more energy.

Each night brought a deserved rest and each morning I woke with blurred eyes and stiff legs. I assumed my body would adapt to the strain. I was better conditioned for cycling than ever before; my legs and core were strong, my mind adaptable. I felt physically capable of taking on the demands of the mountain passes yet still experienced dread each morning about the twelve hours to come.

The impact of the Yellow River – the second-longest in China – was obvious as towns and villages hugged its flanks to take advantage of the fertile soil. A large percentage of China is urbanised but the rural areas still have a significant mass of people. Unlike in Kazakhstan, where I could cycle for days without seeing any real settlement, here it was constant. One village would blend into another, and another; then they would combine to form a town and then a city. It was entirely logical, given the population, but it gave me no relief.

The non-highway roads followed the valleys and rivers. In my golden hour every day when seeking a suitable place for the night, finding a camping spot turned into a creative challenge as almost every square foot of vaguely flat land was farmed and represented somebody's livelihood. A cliff edge with perhaps a small section of cultivated land might hug the road on one side while a steep rock face would rise up on the other.

I would ride on hoping to find somewhere, anywhere, which might give me an element of protection and privacy without disrupting the locals. As much as I did not want to harm the small vegetable patches, I also did not want to be disturbed at sunrise on somebody's land. Often I found myself pitching my tent at the side of the road, in the dark, with my head-torch. Only in the morning would I notice the precariousness of my perch with several hundred metres of empty air a foot to the side of me. Another compromise was under a tree in someone's orchard, usually at an uncomfortably wonky angle. The voices of farmers up surprisingly early were enough to make me spring into action and promptly pack up my life and hit the road, ready for another round of Chinese hide-and-seek that evening.

Needing to avoid farming areas lower down, I would often find a small path or set of steps near the road and park my bike. As in the deep snow in Siberia, it required several journeys to transport my kit, my bike and myself from road level to camping level: a lung-bursting and lactic acid-inducing finale to a day's riding. It was rarely perfect, rather workable, the ground usually just large enough to erect a tent and rest until the morning.

*A typically busy market in Gansu*

The small towns I rode through were bustling and fun, far removed from the slick modern cities, with a consistent variety of street food, loud music, shouting, car horns and pyrotechnics. Every town was also stressful to cycle through because of the constant feeling that someone, or something, was about to make an entirely unexpected manoeuvre. After the solitude and simplicity of the deserts, where I'd had space to think and reflect, it was quite a culture shock. I did my best to adapt but, in terms of other road users in China, the philosophy of 'expect the unexpected' was taken to a whole new level.

Road rage is something we've all likely experienced or witnessed; the same sentiments apply for cyclists but are perhaps heightened due to the exposure and vulnerability. On several occasions, I lost my composure with drivers who indicated one way and then veered off in the opposite direction; or, without any prior warning, made a sudden lurch left or right; or, even worse, slammed on the brakes right in front of me. I did not like my instinctive reactions but they were usually prompted by fear rather than anger. Again, it was a total contrast to Kazakhstan, where the uniqueness of my presence and scarcity of other vehicles meant I had never once felt unsafe among other drivers.

Gansu and Sichuan together would take me several thousand miles into China. My progress was halted for a day after I finally found a bike shop to replace Dorothy's cracked wheel arch and snapped brake cables. Her list of complaints were probably indicative of the stress and sheer weight she had been placed under. It came to a head when the hazardous nature of my situation was made clear on descents from big mountain passes. Each sharp turn required me to hunch down onto my frame and slam my feet into the ground to halt my progress; a method which seriously wore down the rubber on my boots but just about got the job done.

I also took a rest day out of mental fatigue. I arrived at a small town late and wheeled my bike up a hill to find a ledge to sleep on for the night. The spot made for a glorious sunset over the mountains and was in a great position overlooking the town below. The weather had gradually improved and I'd started thinking about wearing sandals again. But next morning I woke to a white-out with a fresh layer of snow settled on the ground around the tent. I had one and a half litres of water, a couple of packs of instant noodles and a few chocolate bars. I did not leave my tent for the next twenty-four hours.

It was an example of where my head and body were at. The toll of the trip was catching up with me. It meant that when things went wrong with the bike, the route or the weather, my mood was dragged further down than I would have expected. Usually I could acknowledge and appreciate the stunning setting I was in but true enjoyment was often beyond me.

---

Just as the physical surroundings changed, so too did the culture and cuisine.

Friends would message and ask about different aspects of the trip they were interested in: the flora and fauna, the people I met, the scenery, what I missed, where I slept, how far and fast I rode, what I listened to, how much it cost, how I communicated and navigated, how often I washed. Each person projected their own passions, their own ideas of achievement and their own hopes and fears about what I was doing.

My sister works in the food industry so was constantly intrigued by my culinary habits. Her expertise and knowledge is immense so I was sure to know what local food to look out for – from yogurt in Bulgaria to *khachapuri* (cheese-filled bread) in Georgia to *lahmacun* (thin flat pizza) and *menemen* (scrambled eggs with tomatoes and peppers) in Turkey. Whatever the region, I got the best advice on the cheapest and most delicious food.

A joy of foreign travel is the scope for sampling different culinary delights. While the success might be questionable in terms of taste – *kumis* in Kazakhstan springs to mind – the experience usually makes it worthwhile. The first actual meal I had in China was a simple fried vegetable and noodle dish. The vibrant colour of the food was the first thing I noticed, followed by the sheer variety of taste sensations compared with the relatively bland flavours in Kazakhstan. The chillies and oils were immediately both noticeable and notable as they hit the back of my throat and made my eyes water, much to the amusement of the waitress. With the bitter cold outside, the hot spices and the sweating they induced was an effective coping method which warmed me up on my break from the bike.

The food across China was a total joy: flavoursome, distinctive and delicious. The thick noodles and rice were, for a cyclist, ideal: maximum calorific gain for minimal cost. Combined with the fresh fruit and street food I came across, my food intake was far healthier than at other stages of the trip when I often got by on nothing more substantial than a pair of baguettes and peanut butter or jam. Cycling in Asia had its perks.

As I progressed through the country, the cuisine changed from region to region and cafe to cafe according to local ingredients, spices and cooking methods. I took photos of various dishes which, I thought, would help when I next ordered. The response when I flashed these photos was either an almost  indignant refusal, a gesture to say that it was not possible or a happy nod of acknowledgement. Yet regardless of people's responses, every meal was different. Indeed my dining experiences, although slightly stressful at times, were always intriguing.

Based on people's recommendations, one place was a must. The dishes of Sichuan are known for their deep, rich flavours, of which the most unique and important spice is the Sichuan pepper. This peppercorn has an intense, fragrant, citrus-like flavour and produces a tingly, pleasantly numbing sensation in the mouth. Sichuan cuisine has a reputation for its wide variety of seasonings and each dish requires different cooking methods. The people have a saying which goes, 'One dish with one flavour, with one hundred dishes comes one hundred flavours.'

I needed a break to wash my clothes and, more importantly, to charge my electronics, so I planned to head to the city of Chongqing. I had done little prior research; it was just another checkpoint on my route south. According to some estimates, it is the largest city in the world with a population of thirty million people if the nine urban and suburban districts are included. That's almost half the population of the UK living in one metropolis.

The size was beyond comprehension. This megacity sprawled and sprawled with giant tower blocks rising up all over the place from miles out. In that way, it reminded me of Istanbul but the buildings were bigger, newer and there were more of them. I stuck to the hard shoulder of the motorway and crossed over the Yangtze – the third-longest river in the world – before stopping on the bridge to look around and try to comprehend the scale of the city. The buildings looked like trees in the Amazon rainforest competing for light and space as more construction work underway made one that bit taller than the cluster around it. The roads crossed over, under and around so I just clung on, stuck to my line, ignored the beeping and hoped I would be okay. After the mayhem of getting there, I arrived at my cheap hostel unrelaxed and, thankfully, unscathed.

I checked in for two nights, long enough to sort all my admin before setting off again. I was in a shared dorm with a typically eclectic bunch that ranged from young Dutch backpackers to a Canadian firefighter and a Mexican hotel owner. I was grateful not only to be able to rest and write but also to find fellow travellers with whom to chat in English and compare stories. My room-mates also accompanied me in sharing one of the region's most famous dishes: Sichuan hot pot.

I had been warned that to eat hot pot alone was a massive social faux pas. Winter is generally seen as the best time of year to eat hot pot, and it was now early February. In a little team of six, therefore, we headed out to a restaurant that had been recommended.

Hot pot, also known as steamboat, is a Chinese cooking method in which a simmering pot of soup stock is prepared at the dining table. It is thought to have originated nearly 1,000 years ago and was eaten by Mongol warriors and horsemen who needed something hot and tasty to keep them warm and nourished. The famous Sichuan style features a dark red broth chock-full and often bristling with twenty spices, chili peppers and mouth-numbing *huā jiāo*, the famous Sichuan pepper. In Beijing, and elsewhere in the north, hot pot broth tends to be on the mild side and, compared to its racy southern cousins, a little bland. In Sichuan it is sharper, spicier and, in the view of many, the 'authentic' hot pot recipe.

*Sichuan hot pot*

After choosing the level of spice for your broth, you select your ingredients, which are traditionally meat and seafood, sliced vegetables and greens, fast-cooking noodles and tofu. The staff told us how long each item would take to cook; it was evident from our confused expressions that we were hot pot virgins. As with fondue, you try to maximise the taste and texture within the broth as you dip and then compliment it with a range of additional spices and sauces. As with *besh-barmak* in Kazakhstan, it is a culinary experience more than merely a meal. It is an exercise in social connectivity, community and conversation. As the saying goes, 'You don't "hot pot" with people you don't like.' I didn't really have much of a choice with whom I 'hot potted' but we had fun, got on well and I was grateful for some light-hearted conversation after having gone a while without it.

## 5.

I had read stories of solo travellers alone in foreign lands and unable to speak the language. I struggled to comprehend how they managed from one day to the next. In China there were *sometimes* English subtitles underneath street signs but, for the first few thousand miles, I remained puzzled. Deciphering roundabouts, street signs and shop names, ordering from menus and shopping for food – things that should have been relatively straightforward became regular and unwelcome daily hurdles to overcome. Adding roaming data to a Chinese SIM or explaining I needed new brake pads for my bike required more creative solutions.

When culture and language are in complete contrast to our norm, our senses are on constant high alert: everything is new and surprising. I observed and tried to understand everything. I wanted to make sense of what was happening around me and why. I spent much of the next few weeks in an almost constant state of intrigue, confusion, admiration, fascination, frustration and fatigue.

Part of the image I had of rural China was of meditative calm, mindfulness, yoga and mountains. Some of the great Western philosophers had appropriated Chinese ideas and discussed how they could be utilised in Western society; I had also read plenty of Chinese philosophy. While it remains prevalent in pockets of Chinese society, what I actually came across was different. Given that Western philosophy and society are not always aligned, perhaps I should not have been surprised by this.

Rarely was my mind able to relax. If it wasn't the driving style – manoeuvre, maybe signal, maybe mirror – then it was the regularity of the spitting everywhere. If it wasn't the fully laden tuk-tuk drivers going to and from the market, then it was the conversation at least ten decibels louder than what I was used to. If it wasn't the fancy-dress parades or megaphones, then it was the fireworks or the slaughtering of pigs. I needed answers for everything.

I was fortunate to be put in touch with Fran, a friend of a friend, who had spent years in rural China as well as in major cities and could explain many of the daily occurrences I was curious about. Through her, so many things which would have remained unexplained or misinterpreted started to make more sense.

Pyrotechnics particularly grabbed my attention, primarily because they were constant and unavoidable. There was no need to set a morning alarm because, if it wasn't a local farmer waking me, it was the noise of nearby fireworks. If I found a camping spot up a hill, I would often find charred gravestones and empty boxes of fireworks nearby. Thankfully, after I had tried and failed to find explanations on the Internet, Fran gave me three primary reasons:

1. All year round, but especially on Tomb Sweeping Day, it is common to release fireworks near the grave of an ancestor to wish their spirits peace in the afterlife, much as we lay flowers. This often means the ground near a grave is charred and littered with firebox streamers. An extension of this is a funeral which can easily be mistaken for a local carnival, celebration or wedding – confusingly, white is also the colour worn at funerals. There was usually little warning before BOOM! and the red tape on the side of the road would erupt. It was certainly a pulse-raiser and stopped me daydreaming.

2. Fireworks make an atmosphere more *rènao*, which roughly translates as 'bustling' or 'lively'. It is more than just the audible element; it is also the general atmosphere and feeling of a place. The same concept explains the incessant sound of car horns, standing shoulder-to-shoulder with people in crowds and edging around others to get to the front of a queue. It is about making China unique, fun and full of life, as opposed to sterile and boring.

3. Chinese New Year took place on 5 February in 2019 as I rode through Sichuan and was a cause of celebration. It was the Year of the Pig, which explained the regularity of pig heads in the market and the sight of pigs having their throats cut and then being bathed and washed in villages as I rode through. Chinese New Year was a lot of fun and a great time to be in the country. The tradition is to return to the rural areas with your family, and the Spring Festival follows. It was a period of smiles, warmth and sunshine; my favourite time in China. Families of all generations spilled out onto the streets and a sense of happiness was present amongst locals that I had not witnessed before.

As I had travelled through Kazakhstan, my choice of route, the historic nomadic culture and inclement weather ensured I regularly met with hospitality, with people usually passing me on to friends, friends of friends and family members across the country. People took my phone number and checked up on me as I ventured east. The Kazakhs I met were pleased I was travelling across their country and doing my best to understand their way of life, language and customs. I was consistently and genuinely humbled there.

In China, the nomadic culture is not as prevalent, so although generous sentiments might have been felt, they were rarely matched by action. There were, in addition, language difficulties and social media restrictions. As a tall, white male, I was viewed as an oddity in the northwest but less so as I moved further south.

Still, there were exceptions. On a particularly cold, misty day near the Sichuan–Guizhou border, I woke with little enthusiasm about the mountain passes ahead but packed up my tent, loaded my panniers and proceeded as always. My fingers and toes were uncomfortable and the moisture in the air ensured I was sodden within fifteen minutes. I sweated up one mountain pass and wrapped up on the descent as the chilly air flew into me. My hands grasped the handlebars and my fingers hovered over the brakes – I was half-expecting the wheels to skid beneath me at any moment on the icy road. I reached the bottom of the descent uncomfortable and shivering but relieved. And then I climbed to another summit and made another nervy descent.

By the time I'd reached the bottom of this second slope, I was even wetter and more uncomfortable than before. My fingers were not responding properly due to the pressure I had exacted on the handlebars going downhill. It was raining heavily so I ducked into a small convenience shop.

The young lady behind the counter, Qing, spotted my discomfort as I bleakly ambled around the aisles looking for nothing in particular. She ushered me to the counter, offered me a seat and placed me next to a heater. I remained in the shop for several hours as Qing kindly dried all my clothes and gave me a selection of hot drinks and noodles. Laboriously, we used her translating app to communicate.

Qing was twenty-two. The shop belonged to her parents but they were out for the day. She had lived in the same village her whole life, as had her parents and their parents before them. She was due to be married the following year to someone in the village and found it highly amusing that I, at the age of twenty-nine, was neither married nor had children. Where she was from in China, she explained, people did not really have much choice in such things; her parents had found her someone suitable to wed. She had never left the area she'd grown up in, had never met someone from Europe before. She laughed coyly when she said I looked like Justin Bieber.

I did not ask for help but she offered it to me, a stranger with whom she could not speak. It was, in the grand scheme of things, perhaps a small gesture that caused her minimal inconvenience but it also gave her minimal outside credit – often a key motivating factor for people's charity. She would likely never meet me or speak to me again. But she took it upon herself to show compassion to an odd-looking foreigner. I left her shop in the afternoon buoyant and positive about humanity. Incidents like this with Qing were a rarity, but even more appreciated as a result.

Another time, having purchased a small bag of clementines – an essential, and appreciated, part of my nutritional routine in China – I was buying a few pieces of fried tofu from a street-food vendor amidst the buzz and *rènao* of a small market when the lady, knowing nothing about me, gestured for me to enter her home next door for food. I gratefully accepted. I warmed up next to her stove, was fed a beautiful curry with rice and chatted to members of her family. There were four generations living under the same roof – taking personal care of elderly family members is essential in China. I was given a small plastic bag of snacks – fried tofu and apples mainly – and sent on my way with a big wave and smiles.

A final incident took place in Guangxi in southern China. The weather had improved and I sat near a river, blissfully zoned out with sunshine hitting my face, while I listened to the bird calls around me.

Two young locals passed by on their bikes. I gave them a small wave, they smiled back and off they went. I thought nothing more of it. Fifteen minutes later, I set off and passed them a mile down the road. They held something out for me as I approached but I noticed too late and my grab was unsuccessful. I was curious as to their motivations: they could have been trying to give me something but equally they could have been wanting to sell me something. Feeling rested and motivated after my stop by the river, I continued on at a fair pace. Remarkably, a few miles down the road, I heard a bell behind me and turned to see the two boys cycling towards me at full pelt. I slowed down, they handed over two cans of Red Bull, said 'Good Luck', and then left. I rode away uplifted and grateful.

Introvert or extrovert, culturally sensitive or painfully ignorant, socially insecure or totally adaptable – we all have our
strengths and weaknesses. It's what makes us human and
makes our characters all the more unique. Perhaps it was
arrogant of me, but the actual cycling and physical challenges
were never major concerns prior to the trip. Of course, if the
elements are unforgiving, it makes it less comfortable, but I
had confidence my body could do what I required of it.

The aspect that worried me most was the social one. I knew
the trip would force me into situations and places where I
was not comfortable, where I felt the obvious outsider and
where I would have to fumble my way along.

Having large numbers of people I do not know, and cannot
communicate with, staring at me day after day was hard to
ignore. People watching me eat every mouthful of a meal was
especially undesirable. I would try to smile it off and present
myself with dignity and composure – shows of outward
displeasure are hugely frowned upon in China – but I found
it a challenge. I knew that people's staring and curiosity were
rarely due to malice but its intrusiveness made me uneasy.
Unless it was necessary, therefore, I became hesitant to stop.

I had never been in such a position before. It was not just a
question of race, gender, age, physique, hair colour, hair style,
language or mannerisms; it was everything. I was a total
peculiarity. I felt like a zoo animal, a fish in a fishbowl, as
people stared intently from afar, pointed and laughed. Rather
than asking for selfies, as had happened in other countries I'd
visited, groups of people would walk right up to me and take
a photo at close range without warning, and without asking.
It happened at almost every restaurant and every stop, every
day. I felt insecure and unwelcome.

I wanted to do anything I could to make it stop, to not be such an abnormality. I had been growing a beard – it was awful but I concluded it had to be tried at least once in life. I had been told by Fran and others that, in China, beards were always viewed with fascination. Perhaps the beard was the cause of my problems; or, at least, a key element without which my life would be made exponentially easier.

I pedalled to an accessible flowing river – many were still frozen over – parked my bike, pulled out a razor and shaved for the first time in six months. I did a social media poll about whether it was the correct decision and the results were conclusive with the vast majority thankful it was gone.

Clean-shaven, I was ready to be accepted by Chinese society. Unsurprisingly, however, the impact was negligible. I continued to be stared at, laughed at, pointed at and photographed continually.

As with the harassment in Xinjiang, I was sometimes disappointed with my own reaction to being treated as a tourist attraction. Sometimes, in restaurants, I turned my back on everyone and faced the wall. Sometimes I walked up to people and pretended to take photos of them a metre from their face, as they had done to me. Sometimes I gesticulated to make it clear enough that I did not like photos being taken. Sometimes I said 'Qǐng méiyǒu zhàopiàn', 'No photos, please.' Sometimes, if I was yet to order, I just got up and left.

My inability to communicate fully, combined with the unexpected plethora of attention, added to the unfortunate conundrum of craving solitude while experiencing loneliness. Reflecting back upon my actions, they seem excessive, almost absurd. But given the stress, the location, the time of year, my experiences in Xinjiang, and having nobody else to talk to and share the experience with, I believe my actions were excusable. When sleep-deprived, cold and hungry in a foreign country, some difficulties can be overburdening but shaking the stability of my own social foundations was a reason I had chosen to come on the trip alone.

## 6.

I had left sunny Hampshire in August 2018 after a summer of football World Cup drama, romance, writing and socialising in the knowledge of what lay ahead. I knew, given my departure date, winter would hit me hard. But I was now heading towards Southeast Asia and, with it, tourists, beaches and friends.

Winter had sapped my spirit. I missed sleeping with bare feet. I wanted to wake up with my tent roof not covered in condensation, my water not frozen. I wanted to cycle without a jacket and not need to wheel my arms around while pedalling to generate heat in my fingertips. I missed Vitamin D and being under the warm rays of the sun.

Since October, I had been wearing my cheap Kazakh boots. Yes, the buckles had broken off, the soles had worn down from using them as brakes on some steep Chinese descents and they had developed a distinctive scent. Yes, they required a bit of massaging every morning to allow my feet to fit into them after an overnight freeze. But they had survived the fiendishly cold winter with temperatures down to -40°C. They had survived some mud, sand and sleet as well.

I had made it through winter and could switch footwear again. I had formed an emotional attachment to my boots but I was ready to let go. The cracks in our relationship had started to form. Perhaps they wanted to hold on and make it work but, emotionally, I had checked out. The sun was shining and, after a long sweaty ascent, I decided the time had come. I had sent the ominous text nobody wants to receive: 'We need to talk.'

So up in the air they went, the hurler both relieved and gleeful. I changed my pedals over, unpacked my sandals, hopped on the bike and felt the reassuring click as my cleats found their old home and my feet were free.

For everybody else who saw it online, it was an amusing photo with a pleasing backdrop. For me, it was much more. It was a moment I had thought about repeatedly, almost more than getting to Vietnam or Singapore. Those were clear goals to keep me moving but I knew if I could get through winter then I could probably get to wherever I wanted.

––––––––

Like many of the best-laid plans, my idealistic, serenely enjoyable final stint through China did not happen. The weather took a fiendish turn. In the space of a few days it went from winter to sunshine to a very confused state of murkiness, cold and mist.

Initially it was just a severe drop in temperature. It was raining heavily and darkness had set in so I found a spot next to a stand of bamboo near the highway. When putting up a tent, continual rainfall is the absolute worst scenario, more difficult to endure than wind, snow or cold. I woke shivering. Frost lined my tent; something I'd missed about as much as conversations with the Xinjiang police. I looked at my bike and even she looked unhappy. As had happened a few weeks before, I concluded I was not going anywhere. I had enough water, noodles and battery charge to sustain me so I just lay there reading, listening to music and feeling a bit sorry for myself again. The following morning, the thermometer edged above zero and I staggered out of my tent, climbed onto my bike and continued south.

What began as a set of roadworks and a short diversion around a collapsed tunnel led to a few hundred miles where I said goodbye to smooth riding. My speed dropped dramatically as I edged my way around potholes, rocks and puddles. Thick, gloopy mud across the road clogged my tyres, chain and derailleur. My estimated timing for crossing the border into Vietnam went up in smoke as my distance per day halved.

I was angry not only for myself but also because I knew this small road, an essential one for so many of the small villages, would not be fixed anytime soon. There was a new two-tiered toll road on the other side of the valley with huge concrete pillars descending to the ground hundreds of feet below.

For months I had reeled off major cities marking my rough route through China: Urumqi, Lanzhou and Chongqing. Those places that had appeared so unachievably far away when I began were now behind me.

I had had visions of crossing the border from Xinjiang to Gansu and finding everything different in one great, dramatic change of scene. Of course, it didn't happen that way. Topographical, social and cultural shifts emerge slowly within a country. On a bicycle, I experienced the transition gently as sights, smells, tastes and sounds trickled into my consciousness.

The shifts were undeniably happening as I headed south, far from the vast emptiness of the desert into lusher, more fertile landscapes. Once again, I began to take pleasure in the smaller things. I sat and watched the world go by as farmers tilled their crops in the sunshine against a backdrop of mountains, rivers flowed free of ice, birds chirped joyfully and pastoral aromas filled my nostrils. Once again, endless straight highways gave way to precarious switchback mountain roads that demanded maximum effort from my legs and lungs. I was able to stand atop peaks looking down at roads I had ridden, and gaze at the scenery lying in wait.

As I pedalled through villages, I saw groups of old men dressed all in black surrounding pairs of friends playing checkers. I saw tuk-tuks and horse-drawn carts taking animals and fruit to and from the market. I saw women sitting outside their little shops and children playing in the streets. Each time anyone saw me, they would stop and stare with the same look of astonishment and fascination. Then they would turn and look at each other as if to say, 'Did you just see what I saw?' Meanwhile I was off, the crazy, tall white man on a bike with all the bags on it. Another village would be around the corner.

These were the signs of progress I had been looking forward to. Gradual alterations in my surroundings provided small dopamine hits and added incentive for the following day. I was beginning to enjoy riding again.

*A change of scenery and pace of life in Guangxi*

When thunder and lightning had struck in eastern Europe, when the bitter cold took over on the Kazakh Steppe, when the police stopped me in Xinjiang, I had questioned what I was doing. I had to be brutally honest with myself about why I was here, what made me leave the safety of home and choose to live this life of a rolling stone.

You have to place your belief in the journey. It is right to question, it is right to challenge your beliefs and learn about why others might not want to do the same. But you also have to commit and commit hard, not just dip your fingers and flee. If you don't fully commit, you'll never fully succeed. Roald Dahl said, 'If you are interested in something, no matter what it is, go at it at full speed ahead. Embrace it with both arms, hug it, love it and become passionate about it.'

When you have those down hours, days or even weeks, you have to remind yourself of the journey you've been on. So often I lost perspective of where I was, and where I had begun, such was the temporary focus on where I was going – the next break in the journey, the next place to unwind and rest. In this case, it was the Vietnamese border. Absurdly, I often lost track of the fact that the 10,000 miles from London to where I was here in China was something to be proud of. Sometimes taking stock was enough to force me to clamber back on the bike and start turning the pedals. To where and what, I was never quite sure.

My new perception of distances was made clear when I caught myself thinking, 'Just the length of the UK to go now.' Here in southern China, the idea of 'almost there' being Land's End to John O' Groats was both amusing and apt. It was, given how far I had come thus far, eminently achievable.

I always believed it was all possible; I had to. I had to have an internal conviction I *could* leave home, I *could* cycle across Europe, I *could* cycle across Kazakhstan and across China. Believing did not mean it was necessarily going to happen, and it certainly didn't mean it was going to be easy, but it did mean the journey was definitely possible.

───

The weather finally cleared and I had renewed momentum. Vietnam was only a day away. I went into a convenience shop, purchased a couple of beers and found myself a pleasant camping spot atop a little hill. I thought about China, about the past few months and what lay ahead.

The next day I descended a steep road through a forest and arrived at the border. The sun was shining and Vietnam was right there, a matter of metres away. I spoke to a border guard.

'Hello, I am trying to go into Vietnam today. Is this the border crossing?'

'Yes, this is correct.'

'Great news, thank you. Where can I enter then?'

'Through that gate. But where are you from?'

'I am from England. I have just cycled across China.'

'No, you cannot proceed. This border is just for Chinese and Vietnamese citizens. You need to go to Friendship Pass. It is the crossing from Pingxiang to Dong Dang.'

'And there is definitely no way I can cross here? Where is Pingxiang? What's the best route there?'

'No. You cannot cross here. Leave now. Thank you. Goodbye.'

I was slightly aggrieved, did a U-turn and cycled back up the hill with slightly less celebratory music playing as I tried to work out where on earth Pingxiang was. It was 200 hilly miles away. I reckoned if I cycled efficiently, I could get there the day after next.

I covered the distance without drama as the temperature shifted up to a ridiculous 20°C.

The new landscape was incredibly picturesque, some of the most beautiful countryside I had seen. Rice paddies and little tractors pulling carts of bamboo appeared amongst extraordinary spikes of rock hundreds of metres high with trees and plants painting everything green. I took photos of flowers and reciprocated smiles and waves from locals wearing wide-brimmed wicker hats.

Perhaps I had needed the closed border to experience a few days of peace before Vietnam. I had been so rushed before – totally focused on where I was going, not present in where I was. Ironically, the detour was the best thing that could have happened.

I arrived at the Pingxiang crossing in better spirits, attained my free two-week visa for Vietnam and wheeled my bike into a new country. There were no bag checks, no imposed phone scans, no photos deleted from my laptop, no police interviews.

As I crossed the line and had my passport stamped, the border guard said, '*Xin chào*. Hello, Mr Stew-art. You have many bags; a big journey. I hope you have a good time in Vietnam. Welcome to our country.' He smiled and shook my hand.

In no way could I process the past few months in China and Kazakhstan. It had been tough. I was still yet to see another cyclist and I still had a while until I saw a friend in Laos. But it was a big moment. I felt liberated. In my mind, Vietnam was safe space.

———

I had been told by an expert on Chinese culture before I entered the country:

> There is good China and there is bad China. I have little doubt, given the route you're taking, that you will experience both. I am not going to tell you what to think, you are old and mature enough to make your own evaluations based on your

own intuition, reading and experiences. I will, as always, be
extremely interested in what your thoughts are when you get
out the other side.

China had tested me in almost every way possible. I had
never felt more alone in such a crowded place. The country
had made me embarrassed, angry, resentful and confused; it
had also, and equally, impressed, inspired and fascinated me.
My mind had been restless from the first day to the last. I had
learned something new every day.

I left China more interested in the country than when I'd
arrived. It had taught me aspects of foreign travel which
might have remained unknown had I been anywhere else or
with anyone else. It was an extreme; not just the scenery and
landscapes but the society and culture.

I look back now with a degree of antipathy and sadness. Part
of me wishes I'd been mentally stronger so I would not have
been so affected by everything outside my control. I suppose,
it showed the flaws and weaknesses in my character as much
as it showed some strengths.

If I had been with a friend, I'm confident that much of the
intensity of certain situations would have been diffused. Sir
Edmund Hillary said he 'regarded a sense of humour as one
of the most important things on a big expedition.' He was
right, of course.

Over the years I have been on many expeditions with a whole
range of people in different situations, from jungles and
deserts to high altitude and oceans. Invariably, humour was
our instantaneous release valve when the pressure was rising.
It was something I lacked in China. I had needed an inappropriate joke and banter at my own expense for the life I had
chosen to live. I had too much time to internalise the light-

hearted comments I received from several thousand miles away and the impact was wasted even when the intent was positive.

The journey taught me about things I truly valued when they were so dearly lacking: kindness, communication and love. If nothing else, those three very basic qualities, which had already been significant to me before the trip, were of far greater importance now. The experience remains with me and will continue to shape my perspective on a number of aspects of my own life. For that, I'm grateful.

During the latter part of my time in China, I had listened to the 1990s D:Ream song, 'Things Can Only Get Better' almost on repeat. It had kept me optimistic, acting as a reminder that a turn in the road was coming, the following day would be different and that things would improve. Singapore was very much my aim: the end of mainland Asia. I had friends and family waiting there. But for now, I had made it to Southeast Asia, to Vietnam and had convinced myself that weeks of sunshine, socialising and sand lay ahead.

# PART V

## GRATITUDE

*For me, exploration was a personal venture... I set myself a goal on these journeys, and, although the goal itself was unimportant, its attainment had to be worth every effort and sacrifice.*

— WILFRED THESIGER

# 1.

Relief is a wonderful feeling, the release from emotional and physical toil, the alleviation of discomfort, struggle and anxiety. Perhaps it was merely psychological, perhaps it was assisted by a rich coffee at the first cafe I saw, or perhaps it was the cheerfulness of the people I met after crossing the border. Regardless, there was an immediate feeling of comfort in Vietnam.

I spent my first night in the country at a cheap *nhà nghỉ*, or guesthouse; I felt I deserved a treat. The people received me warmly and offered to wash my clothes – I hope as a result of the mud rather than the smell. I wandered to the only restaurant in the village and ordered a beer alongside an uncomplicated vegetable and chicken dish the waitress suggested. Shortly after finishing my meal, I was ushered over to a table of high-spirited folk, given another beer and a shot of I don't know what. One of the people spoke a version of English and we fumbled through, making connections where we could and drinking merrily.

'Ah, you support Newcastle. Black and White. St James' Park. Alan Shearer. The best number nine!'

'Oh, the glory days,' I said in response.

I was often amazed at the local people's knowledge in discussions of football. Sometimes they would just say the one name again and again, such as 'Alan Shearer', and I would nod enthusiastically while recreating his famous raised right arm celebration. Football was almost always a bond in Vietnam. In China, I had been grateful to utilise my random assortment of NBA knowledge to form a bond, smiling and exchanging names, from LeBron James and Yao Ming to Michael Jordan and Dennis Rodman. Sport was a commonality allowing for mutual appreciation.

The night went on. Shots of homemade beer continually came my way. In Vietnam it is customary to shake to hands with the person toasting you, and everyone wanted to toast the random cyclist, so a lot of alcohol went down and a lot of handshakes ensued. Everyone's spirits were high as we laughed, drank and ate. The people here were accepting of me, never once making me feel uncomfortable. It immediately gave me a warm feeling and reminded me of my vodka-fuelled final night in Kazakhstan with the truck drivers. The result in the morning was much the same: a slightly hazy head, a gentle easing onto the pedals and a few strong coffees to get the legs going.

Life in Vietnam continued in a positive vein. I stayed in several cheap *nhà nghỉ*, ended up in a number of karaoke bars with locals and made quick progress in learning the local ways. The daylight hours were longer, the temperature lovely, the scenery appealing, the food delicious and the atmosphere upbeat. I was happy. The weight on my shoulders about the ordeal ahead, something significantly impacting my mental state, was lifted. I was relieved. I took more videos and spoke to people back home who could sense the change in my outlook.

From children, parents and grandparents, I heard '*chào*' or '*xin chào*' all the time. People waved, smiled and rode alongside me. I could see schoolgirls giggle sheepishly as I rode past and then try to follow me as I whizzed away. My bike was lighter, I was lighter after China, but I felt strong. I was near the coast and the roads were fast and flat. I didn't even mind when they became crumbly and dusty; it was almost expected.

G. K. Chesterton said, 'The traveller sees what he sees, the tourist sees what he has come to see.' Travel by bike or on foot, without a specific route, and you start to sense small trends of everyday life instead of curated attractions. You see the gender roles and social dynamics in small villages. You learn the decorum of dining as a guest, the types of farming equipment, what cars people drive, what sport the children play, how weddings are celebrated, what truck drivers eat and the hours people work. You gain an insight into what might constitute normal life for the people who live there.

───

Winding my way through the valleys and over the mountains in the west of the country, day-to-day life was simplified. There were no guesthouses so I wild camped again. This became a challenge due to the prevalence of rice paddies, where the ground was heavily saturated and wholly unsuitable for a tent. The other option, as always, was staying with locals. I remained extremely reticent to ask anyone for help unless it was wholly necessary. When it did happen, it was always a rewarding and memorable experience.

I was riding through tall forests with nothing but the sound of bird calls and the gentle rolling of rubber on tarmac in my ears. The day was coming to a close but I was content riding and not overthinking the following day. I came to a village and no shop was in sight so I headed to a small hospital-type building and found a way of communicating with the man who appeared to be in charge. I was kindly offered a shower and bed for the night.

In the meantime, I went to watch a five-a-side football game while the sun was setting and I was stretching off. I must have looked a peculiar sight and was soon invited to join in. The game was played with bare feet and jumpers for goal posts: old school. My significant height advantage was gratefully received by my teammates and we reverted to a 'route one' tactical approach in search of a late winner, having clawed our way back from 2–0 down courtesy of a few controversial refereeing decisions. The tactics paid off and a typically shambolic goalmouth scramble ensured a gritty 3–2 victory in extra time.

I had missed the simple fun and cohesion that playing sport brings. Team sport has been a fundamental part of my life, so I loved being welcomed in this small mountain village. The victory and a respectable performance was a bonus. If nothing else, it meant supplies of homemade beer were plentiful after the whistle blew for full-time. I was invited to join a few of the players for dinner afterwards. Sweaty but pleased, we sat outside, cross-legged on a beautifully patterned rug, in the mildest of temperatures. Stir-fried vegetables, rice, bread and a pork curry hit the spot perfectly. The *gỏi cuốn* (light, fresh spring rolls) to start and *bánh tiêu* (Vietnamese doughnut) to finish bookended another charming evening.

Going through the small villages in the mountains was a true highlight. The odd fully laden bus would whizz by but otherwise it was bicycles, scooters and animals. Cows, bulls and pigs showed zero intent to shift out the centre of the road while chickens, dogs, ducks and goats ran in all directions at the first sight of this weird, silent, two-wheeled beast.

*Exploring rural Vietnam*

Despite the gradually improving economy in Vietnam – broad-based growth, low inflation, ease of international business development and less debt – there are still some seriously poor areas. I found the low noise, homemade wooden houses on stilts and simple lifestyle very appealing. Compared with the frantic lowland towns I had been through, it was such a peaceful process just pootling along and listening to the sounds, observing the nature and people around me. I only met with gentleness. Once again, it made me think about the places I valued in my own country: countryside as opposed to city, fields as opposed to skyscrapers, trees as opposed to street lights, birds as opposed to buses.

Being in the tropical zone, Vietnam was heaven when it came to fresh fruit. *Dứa* (pineapple), *chuôî* (banana), *vú sữa* (star apple), *bưởi* (pomelo), *quýt* (mandarin) and durian were all refreshing and delicious. The colours, tastes and health benefits were a constant source of excitement. When it came to biking boosters, though, one thing in Vietnam was tough to match. Coffee culture, most famously in the capital Hanoi, is a serious business and something I wholeheartedly embraced. As in Italy, the sunshine-filled espresso breaks mid-cycle were a great pleasure.

The blend of beans used and the preparation process gives Vietnamese coffee a distinctive taste. The finely ground, dark roasted beans go into a *phin* or traditional drip filter which sits atop a small glass. Hot water is added and the rich coffee trickles down. The real secret lies in the sweetened condensed milk and ice that blend together to make it an absolute gem when cycle touring. I called this combination of caffeine and sugar 'Vietnamese Rocket Fuel'. *Cà phê sữa đá* (Vietnamese iced coffee) was an addictive and delicious treat: I cannot recommend it enough. Alongside my Vietnamese playlist – which included Creedence Clearwater Revival, Edwin Starr, Buffalo Springfield and Bob Dylan – it meant I pedalled with almost constant vigour and determination.

I was not expecting to develop such a soft spot for the country and stayed longer than planned. It was the perfect antidote, though. I believe I could have visited it any time and come away with the same feelings. The aspects I'd foreseen lived up to expectations. But it was things I had not anticipated – the positivity, food, coffee, scenery and the joy the rural communities brought me – that made the biggest difference.

I've always thought the greatest influence on my state of mind and temperament are the natural surroundings I find myself in: mountains, deserts, forests or rivers. Yet China had all that and more; it was one of the most beautiful and diverse countries I have ever visited. Still, although its beauty gave me a lift at times, it did not come close to the pleasure I experienced in Vietnam. Having squads of people on scooters catch up with me after I'd overtaken them, to simply say hello and smile, was wonderful. When I saw the faces of schoolchildren in the countryside brighten up just because they saw me on my bike, it was impossible not to want to smile back.

The final fifteen miles before the border with Laos were spent grinding up a seemingly never-ending mountainside. I sweated profusely, wearing just sandals, a T-shirt and shorts. It was 40°C. Only a few weeks before, it had been 40°C cooler. Not long before that, it had, almost unbelievably, been another 40°C cooler. An 80°C temperature swing in a matter of months. My body was too confused to know how to react. I was happy, however, with an overdue and intense Vitamin D hit, knowing a border crossing and a chance to cool off lay at the summit.

As I tackled the final few miles, I pedalled through a small village. My speed was minimal and sweat levels were high in the humid tropical climate. I was switching between standing on my pedals while pulling on the handlebars and then sitting back to focus on different muscle groups in my legs. As I passed some children at the side of the road, they ran alongside me en masse, smiling and waving. The video I took recalls one of my favourite moments of the whole trip; it signifies so much of what I loved about Vietnam. The country gave me everything I had needed. The video was a snapshot of what I wanted to remember the country by and, as my final memory, it would be the image I took with me to the border and beyond.

**2.**

'We saw your bike and you sitting here so thought we'd say hi.'

I was happily sitting in a small roadside cafe with a bowl of *pho*. They were hunched over the handlebars of their heavily laden touring bikes as I had done so many times before. They both wore loose-fitting T-shirts, shorts and sandals. Sweat shone on their brows and they had big smiles on their faces. They looked the sort of travellers you might hope to find in a mountain village in rural Laos.

This was Elis and Lukas, a Dutch couple who had spent eighteen months meandering 10,000 miles from the Netherlands to Southeast Asia, having got married just before they set off on this grand adventure. We exchanged pleasantries about where we were from, where we had been and where we were going. From that information, you can evaluate so many things. My own route choice indicated a desire for solitude and extreme conditions. Elis and Lukas had taken the traditional route across Central Asia at the recommended time of year and, moving at a reasonable pace, had been accompanied by other cyclists for vast swathes of their trip. When you weigh up such basic information so early in an encounter, you can be right or wrong but such quick calculations become a necessary skill for establishing safety and companionship.

They immediately went to the market to find cheap local food before returning and joining me for lunch. Both they and I were on tight budgets; like me, they camped most of the time. We were all also part of the same WhatsApp group. Just that morning, I had seen a photo pop up of Elis, with her arms aloft, against a gorgeous green mountain backdrop. The caption read 'Happy International Women's Day everyone'. I did not know who she was, nor the person who took the photograph. Seeing them a few hours later was sheer coincidence and a great excuse for an extended break.

For me, Elis and Lukas represented far more than just a pair of European cyclists on a similar journey. They were the first cycle tourers I had seen in over five months and 7,000 miles, thanks to my detour. I knew other cyclists were out there, within a few thousand miles and a few months, but nobody was on my exact route and nobody else was idiotic enough to do it over winter.

They had German friends who were staying at a small guesthouse in the next town, about thirty miles away. None of us were keen to pay for accommodation but we also lacked a suitable reason to say no. We had washed in rivers the day before but the thought of a bed and a few beers was too appealing to refuse. It was all the motivation we needed and, after cooling down and freshening up under the shade from the midday sun, we set off together and headed south.

*Riding in the Laos hills with Elis and Lukas*

Halfway up a long ascent, we encountered a French couple, Jean-Pierre and Marie. Jean-Pierre and I admired each other's clip-in sandals; sometimes amongst our touring community, it's the smallest things that create a sense of familiarity.

'It's like London buses on these roads,' I quipped.

'What do you mean, London buses? We are in Laos, *non*?'

'It's a typical British expression, sorry. You say "like London buses" when you wait a long time for something and then several come at once. I have not seen a cyclist for 7,000 miles and now I've seen four in the space of a few miles.'

'*Bien*. The London buses I like. Marie and I have been to London before. I know what you mean by the waiting. But you English like to queue, *non*? Maybe that is why you like the London buses.'

We spent the evening idly chatting and comparing travel stories at the guesthouse. Shared experiences offer a pleasant reassurance. We discussed similarities and differences in our routes, equipment, lifestyles and challenges. We deliberated over future plans, great and small. We discussed the best and worst bits of our trips. Often the really tough bits, the extremes, could not be adequately put into words, but we could each visualise what the others meant from our own experiences.

Still, some things were unique. They had experienced vast sections of the Uzbekistan desert in 50°C heat. I had had freezing temperatures in Siberia. The internal suffering and longing for a change were comparable. There was mutual respect between us; an understanding of what it actually takes to embark on this sort of trip. We knew the reality of what packing your life into a few bags and setting off from home really means.

We parted ways in the morning. I was heading south, the Germans heading off by train, the Dutch staying for another night and the French heading west.

I thought about the last time I had seen other cycle tourers, on the Goderdzi Pass in Georgia. I had been sweating my way up the rocky, muddy track when three people on bikes came hurtling my way. They stopped and laughed when they saw me. Mud was splattered all over their bikes, their panniers and their faces; they were every inch the image of youthful, joyous adventurers. It turned out they were Americans. We exchanged basic information about what the route ahead was like.

'Good luck up there, man, it's tough. It's pretty gnarly and cold with a strong wind and the road turns to shit.' They were grateful to be on their way down, while I had many hours ahead of going up. We parted ways with handshakes, wishing each other the best in our respective travels.

That had been Day 50. I never imagined it was the last time a cycle tourer would cross my path for another 165 days.

Arriving in a new country became an odd routine that tore my emotions in opposite directions. I looked ahead to a land of new possibilities and stories, especially in countries I knew little about. Crossing a border also meant leaving a place to which I had become accustomed. It could make me reluctant to up sticks and move. To leave is to embrace uncertainty.

Out of respect for the country you're in, you need to learn and try to adapt to local traditions. In the first few days, there is much to take in. My brain would buzz as it tried to amass knowledge quickly so as to avoid the obvious mistakes that foreigners make. Learning forms of introduction, basic vocabulary and particular gestures is one aspect of this; getting to grips with family dynamics, religious beliefs and political inclinations is another. Then you must learn exchange rates, road signs, driving styles, the price of staple items and the names of different types of food.

Laos is more obviously Buddhist than its bordering countries. The economy in Laos is dwarfed by that of Vietnam. The amount of tourism is also markedly less than in Vietnam, especially in the mountains, and accessibility for visitors, other than in the lower valleys, can be a significant challenge. I was very much in the mountains. The hills were steeper and the roads in worse condition than in Vietnam. The children smiled, waved and shouted '*sabaidee*' with great enthusiasm – literally meaning 'It goes well'. This is a form of greeting you hear everywhere. There is a pleasing simplicity in village life in the Laos hills with 80 per cent of rural Laotians making their living from rice fields and subsistence farming.

The muggy atmosphere and serious heat meant I had to be up early to take advantage of the cooler temperatures, rest at lunch and set off again in late afternoon. That was the theory. In practice, I often got up later than planned after a sweaty night somewhere in a tent and rode exasperated through the midday heat.

Navigation was simple: follow Road Number 7 west for several hundred miles, take a left and then head south on Route 13 towards Vientiane. This was another thing off my mind. Instead, I could marvel at the magnificent forested mountain ranges extending far and wide with a hazy blue shimmer on the horizon from the overhead sun.

Poor Dorothy was in serious need of some love. As I am all too aware, and say to others, prevention is better than a cure. The phrase, 'Do as I say, not as I do', also comes to mind. I had gone several thousand miles with the same chain in a whole range of conditions and terrains. As a result, the links on the chain had gradually stretched, which placed extra tension on the teeth of the cassette so that eventually the links no longer fitted snugly into the gaps. The grinding sound started to become a serious issue. Big hills also add tension as they require more power.

In a nutshell, I lost a new gear almost every day as the teeth of the cassette wore down and the chain links stretched. When a steep hill appeared before me, I had to use as much momentum as I could to get up to a point where I could peddle no more, whereupon it was a matter of hopping off and pushing the bike to the top. It became a tiresome habit. My ego was also slightly dented as it implied to drivers I was unable to ride up the hill due to its gradient. As my mum would have told me, 'A bit of humble pie never does anyone any harm.'

I did, on a few occasions, find a sneaky solution to this. Trucks usually have enough power to head up hills at a reasonable speed. Less powerful trucks often chugged up the steeper hills grunting and groaning but certainly quicker than me pushing my bike. As they approached, I would mount my bike, hold onto the right handlebar and grab the truck with my left hand. I then very happily got a free lift. At the top, I would usually have enough momentum to overtake them and fly down the other side. Without exception, I was met with a friendly poop of the horn and a big wave from the driver. I think they rather respected my boldness.

Was it cheating? I believed wholeheartedly in pedalling every bit I could. However:

a. My only other choice was pushing the bike.

b. Technically, I was still on my bike.

c. It was not an easy manoeuvre. I didn't get it right every time and it required a significant amount of poise and bike control to get into position, make the grab and then hold on as the truck weaved its way up the hill.

Cheating or not, it was good fun and well worth the effort.

---

The flat fifty-mile approach through the Mekong Valley to the capital is infamous amongst cyclists. The heavy flow of trucks meant it was hot, dusty and stressful as red dirt continually got chucked up into my sticky, sweaty face. I was marginally bothered but no more; my focus was my destination, despite being down to a solitary gear. It was a nervy stretch but I secretly enjoyed the challenge and the test of personal resourcefulness in finding a solution to the problem. My excitement started to reach dizzy levels as I got closer to Sophia's house in Vientiane.

I hadn't seen a familiar face on the road since Tbilisi, over five months before. I had met wonderful people along the way but it wasn't the same. Sophia was an old friend of mine, now a teacher in the city.

I followed her directions. She said it would be obvious which house was hers. A printed A4 sign on the gate made me laugh. It was a stupid old photo of me with the caption:

> Dearest Vagabond,
> This way for shelter, biscuits & beer.
> S xx

Sophia was still at work, so I made myself at home, showered, put on a clothes wash and stretched.

Finally, the front door opened and I was greeted with a big hug.

I didn't know I had missed hugs, but I had. I didn't know how much I had missed my friends, but I had. Here was someone who had known me a long time and who genuinely valued and appreciated me, not as a travelling cyclist who needed help, but as a person and a friend. I don't think she knew how much it meant but it didn't matter. She was just being her enthusiastic self and, right then, I valued this more than anything.

Within a few hours of my arrival, Sophia and I visited a traditional Laos sauna. We showered, donned our sarongs, massaged ourselves with a ground-coffee-and-yogurt mixture, and rinsed ourselves off with a jug of water before sweating in the sauna, overheating and going through the process again. It proved a most unexpected, bizarre and – given the condition I was in – welcome addition to my itinerary.

We had a special five days together, often sitting on her balcony with music and a few beers overlooking the Mekong River, the border between Laos and Thailand. Other times, we went exploring around the city with me on the back of her scooter. We drank, ate pizza, went to karaoke bars, spoke to friends back home, watched movies and mused over travel experiences. I gave a talk on my trip to her school class. Feelings of confusion, boredom, amusement and fascination are rarely concealed by children so it kept me on my toes and agile in my presentation techniques. I wrote, reflected and relaxed.

I was meant to leave on the Friday morning and cross into Thailand but had little desire to bid farewell. As we went to bed on Thursday, I said, 'If it's okay, I'd rather not go anywhere tomorrow.' I felt happy and safe where I was. The very idea of hitting the road again and camping out by myself had rather lost its appeal. Friday was spent doing more of the same and when evening came, again, I had little desire to get back on the bike at sunrise.

Sophia had to head off early which left me home alone. Without her around, I believed I was now just delaying for the sake of it, out of fear of what lay ahead. The tiresome old phrase, 'The first step is the hardest', sprang to mind – the time had come, the trip must go on. I loaded up my panniers, now marginally lighter since I'd unloaded a few more bits of kit. I hopped aboard Dorothy, who looked much happier with her new crank, cassette and chain, put on my cap and sunglasses, and rolled away. Another difficult departure; a rolling stone once more.

**3.**

Since setting off, I had been so absorbed by the journey – on where I was, my surroundings, the various cultures and lifestyles I encountered – that it and the bike had become my life. I also believe it had to be that way. I had to immerse myself wholeheartedly in what I was doing. If I had approached the stint across Central Asia and China with too much of a glance backwards to the life I had left, or ahead to a future life I wished for, I would not have been able to endure what I did. I would probably have given up.

My reluctance to depart from Sophia's was indicative of a slight change in outlook; my stay in Vientiane brought a lightness I had lacked. It was partly about her, but it was also about what she represented: home, friendship, future, normality. It reaffirmed my view from the start that this was not real life, rather a temporary chapter to embrace, something I would never regret but certainly not the future I sought.

I had a few thousand miles across Thailand and Malaysia to get to Singapore, my real target. More sunshine, sand and smiles should lie the other side of the Mekong. I crossed the Friendship Bridge, went from Lao kip to Thai baht, from a landlocked country to one with nearly 1,800 miles of coastline, from riding on the right-hand side of the road to the left and from a country with seven million people to one with sixty-eight million. I only had a few more weeks left to go.

Despite the welcome distractions of roadside watermelon, pineapple and street food vendors early in Thailand, I still felt slightly subdued having left Vientiane. These sentiments were heightened after an email I received from Sophia which included the lyrics of Bob Dylan's 'Tangled Up in Blue' rewritten to reflect my journey. It was an artistic masterpiece and one which I treasured enormously. Cycling in the unforgiving heat and sweating in my tent at night filled me with little enthusiasm compared to a bed and balcony beers with her. My response, as ever, was to tell myself, 'The trip has to go on.'

I wanted to make a big indentation after having been stationary for almost a week. I pushed hard from Vientiane to Bangkok to cover the 500-mile stretch in four days before stopping for a short visit with a university friend, Freddie, and his wife, Astrid. Again, their companionship, alongside a golf course, a coffee machine, a bed, their puppies and a selection of Lonely Planet travel guides, was hugely valued.

Another thing vying for my roadside attention were the forty candidates for the fast-approaching 2019 Thai general election. It was a fascinating process trying to analyse different people, guessing their policies and making judgements on the image they presented based on their campaign posters. Although initially confused, I was confident I could gain insights and local knowledge from my Warmshowers hosts.

Warmshowers is a reciprocal online cycle-touring community where people offer cyclists their homes to stay in for a night or two. The system is based on trust and mutual acknowledgement of the journey we're on when pedalling through a foreign country with nought but our panniers and a sense of general confusion. I had avoided this site at the start; I wanted to learn to be self-sufficient. Recently my view had changed, however. Beyond the obvious benefits of a bed and shower, it provided a great opportunity to meet up with locals and better understand the environment and culture I was cycling through. I never failed to learn from my hosts, whether it was beers and live music until the wee hours with Manoon, the home cooking of Patty and her mum, Utid Sumlee, or the laughter with Somchai and his wife Kalaya, and never once regretted the experience.

---

Other than the briefest of stints in Laos with Elis and Lukas, I had not ridden with anyone since France. I was accustomed to my own routines, methods and speed. If I slept badly, I lay in my tent an hour more in the morning. If I went to bed early and woke with enthusiasm, I was up and away swiftly. If I felt strong, I rode long and hard. If I felt lethargic, I stopped for longer and reduced my expected distance for the day.

I was having a good morning; the sun was shining and my legs and mind felt strong. Ahead of me appeared another cyclist, panniers either side of his rear wheels, a large bag on his rear rack and a mane of long blonde hair flowing in the wind. I continued at my own pace and caught up with the young chap, whereupon we pulled over and had a little chat. His name was Emil. He was twenty-three, Danish, and, having set out from Scandinavia, had cycled 9,000 miles in twelve months. He intended to continue south to Singapore, then Indonesia, then cross back over the Equator and fly home to a career in healthcare having studied medical science at university.

I saw a lot of my former self in Emil. I was only six years older but for me those are an important six years in which self-understanding and reprioritising are key themes. He, like several other solo cycle tourers I knew, was male, had recently finished studying, had done a bit of travelling and wanted to 'achieve' something of significance where the potential for self-improvement was great and the expenses were little. I respected his journey and was amused by his anecdotes of the trials and tribulations he had faced on his route.

We rode together for a few hours before stopping for lunch. We browsed the menu and ordered an assorted medley of items we liked the look of. What arrived – water and a few rice dishes – was rather different to the beers, *pho* and *pad see ew* we'd anticipated. If I'd been alone, the mix-up might have caused a degree of frustration. As it was, we laughed and ate together. I thought about China and how different it might have been if I'd had company. Those small daily irritations would have been reduced if there had been a calming presence alongside me, with each of us providing a filter for the other's emotions.

After lunch, Emil and I split off, taking different routes on a different schedule to get to our destinations, each habituated by solo travel.

In Thailand, it seemed as though a great pressure had been alleviated. I had covered over 12,000 miles and was enticingly close to my major goal of Singapore. A journey through Malaysia awaited, meeting a friend in Kuala Lumpur would split up the leg, and then I was out of land.

I still rode long hours and long miles but was content stopping to savour fresh fruit juice or coconut water from street sellers. I was happy to take a detour along the shore to enjoy the soothing sound of gentle waves lapping on the sand. It felt a rare privilege to embrace this side of Thailand. For so many hours as I rode, I had thought about swimming off this coast. In my mind, it represented mental calm and relaxation – as opposed, say, to riding midwinter through Urumqi, the most inland city in the world, near the Eurasian Pole of Inaccessibility. I was grateful for the image I had built up of being by the sea and was relieved not to be disappointed by what I found.

Cyclist Doug Bradbury said, 'The best rides are the ones where you bite off much more than you can chew, and live through it.' The idea that I was on holiday, created by the presence of palm trees, sandy beaches and tourists, had a great psychological impact on me. The presence of young backpackers, couples and families gave me reassurance, despite the contrasting types of holidays we were on. The times when I was a true outsider, an irregularity in a strange land, felt like the distant past.

In Thailand, the urban traffic was mad and the touristy spots hectic. The rainstorms were almost biblical in their ferocity and the sun a consistently debilitating presence. And yet, despite these inconveniences, it struck me as truly one of the best places you can cycle tour. The pace of life was slow and stress levels were lower; the costs were manageable and the people friendly. In the way it relaxed my mind, it was everything I'd hoped for.

# PART VI

## REFLECTION

*Remember what Bilbo used to say: It's a dangerous business, Frodo, going out your door. You step onto the road, and if you don't keep your feet, there's no knowing where you might be swept off to.*

— J. R. R. Tolkien

# 1.

I crossed the border into Malaysia and browsed my map for the quickest route to the coast. A taxi driver came up to me and asked where I had come from and where I was going. When I mentioned the UK, he excitedly told me that he had studied at Pembroke College, Cambridge, for six months a few decades before and it remained his favourite place in the world. He shared a few of his memories about the buildings, punting on the River Cam and trips to London. He gave me a few bottles of water and a handful of sweets, and wished me luck travelling around his country. The encounter gave me a positive first impression as I pedalled to the sea once more.

For hundreds of miles, I followed a quiet, winding road hugging the shore a few metres away. In contrast to that serenity, I also got caught out by several explosive tropical rainstorms which saturated most of the perishable items in my leaky front panniers. I had cycled in some shocking weather but Mother Nature had a way of throwing me new curveballs to keep my interest piqued and remind me of who was in charge. Peak wet season – from April to October –

would have made those rainstorms a consistent inconvenience rather than a source of unforeseen amusement as I
sought refuge at cafes, dried my belongings and waited until
they'd passed.

When the weather was more congenial, I had a daily dilemma
about where to stop and eat given the abundance of roadside
cafes and street-food vendors. Malaysia is located along the
ancient spice route and the cultural fusion is manifested in the
variety of food, from Keralan fish curries and smooth coconut
dishes to noodle soups and fried rice variants. Staples like *roti
canai* (flatbread), *rojak* (fruit and vegetable salad), *batu maung
satay* (grilled meat on skewers) and *koay chiap* (duck and
noodle soup) usually hit the spot. I also developed a fondness
for *nasi lemak*, which is rice cooked in coconut milk that comes
in a little banana-leaf package. *Nasi lemak* is traditionally a
breakfast dish but I would stash a few extra to graze on
throughout the day.

The vast array of culinary options is also indicative of the
cultural melting pot within the country. Malaysia is a strik-
ingly multi-ethnic, multicultural and multilingual society,
which was evident from the outset. The original culture stems
from the Malays who constitute more than 50 per cent of the
population. They moved here in ancient times but there is
now a strong influence of Indian, Chinese, Persian and British
cultures all thrown in.

Whereas in Thailand, around 94 per cent of the population is
Buddhist (over sixty million people), in Malaysia there is a
noticeable melange of identities and religions. Although Islam
is the official state religion, the constitution of Malaysia
allows for freedom of worship and the churches, mosques
and temples spread across the country made me reflect back
to previous places I had visited where such liberties were

denied. I heard the country described as 'Asia in miniature' and I could see why. In my short stint there, I slept alongside Buddhist monks on a sleeping mat in a temple, a Christian music teacher, Khim, on the floor in his studio, and in the home of Nilam and her conventional Muslim family.

I experienced a striking encounter shortly before arriving at Nilam's home. I got a puncture from a sharp bit of metal which led to damaged brake pads and a few other issues. Being tired, sweaty and craving progress, it pissed me off. As was often the case, a few people stopped to watch but I just wanted to be left alone to fix what was becoming a tricky problem. A young boy, Amin, headed off and then returned ten minutes later with a pint of water. I was grateful but, still slightly on edge, wished he'd leave me be. Thankfully, he understood my body language and went off. He returned ten minutes later with a coconut, soy milk and crisps.

I could no longer remain irked. I was grateful and spoke to him. He was a bright 11-year-old boy. I asked him why he continued to want to help me even when he knew I was annoyed. In his words, 'The teaching of Allah is to look out for others and help them. We have to act with generosity and thoughtfulness in our one life. I believed you needed help. I hope I was right.'

---

Navigating my way through the giant metropolis of Kuala Lumpur was utter chaos. Not the overly congested six-lane ear-piercing chaos of Istanbul, but rather the confusion produced by a spaghetti-like assortment of major roads criss-crossing in all directions with a regular flow of traffic and zero cycle lanes. I had little clue where I was going or how to get there; it soon appeared that few of the other road users had a clue either. I somehow made it through unscathed and found myself at the base of the Petronas Twin Towers – for me, the architectural symbol of the city. From 1998 until 2004, they were the tallest buildings in the world. They stand at over 450 metres and consist of eighty-eight floors. The protestations from a rather stroppy policeman about where I could wheel my bike fell on my selectively deaf ears.

I heard some English accents so asked a man to take a photo of me. Much to my satisfaction, one of the group had a fish-eye lens to give perspective of the height of the towers.

'So, where have you come from?'

'London.'

'Yeah, but where have you ridden from?'

'London.'

'Sorry, you've cycled here from London?'

'Spot on. Thirteen thousand miles. I wouldn't ask why. I've been asking myself the same question.' He looked dumfounded so I continued, 'Anyway, lovely to chat and thanks for the photo. I'd better be off now or I think our new friend might get a bit upset.'

The policeman had found a few colleagues and was heading my way. I hopped back on Dorothy and fled the scene before getting into trouble with the authorities again.

The real purpose of coming to Kuala Lumpur was to see Linnea, another old and trusted friend.

Such was the amount of time I had spent alone, I had convinced myself that introspective thoughts were a positive thing. They provided a genuine chance to disengage, process information and reflect. While I wholeheartedly believe that, I also wondered about the negative impact of too much time alone.

Without genuine discourse, it is easy to convince yourself of almost anything. I had so much time to think over every scenario and every interaction I had with other people. While riding, and alone in my tent, I would pose theories and ideas to myself before arguing their merits (or lack of) back and forth. My thoughts had become cyclical and repetitive. What I actually needed was someone I trusted to talk to about the small daily things and the random thoughts about where I was. I had regular phone calls with family and friends but it was not the same as them being there. I missed them. I missed the laughter.

I enjoyed meeting and staying with strangers; it never failed to be an enlightening experience. But equally, you can never truly relax. You cannot sit on a sofa with your feet up in front of a David Attenborough series and sip a cold beer as I could with Linnea. You cannot admit to feeling tired or antisocial and be excused for it. When seeing a real friend after being on the road for many miles, those cultural formalities travellers carefully adhere to are not required; you can simply chat without being judged or scrutinised.

However far and long I continued on this journey, parting with friends was hard. Knowing you're hitting the road again and turning over the pedals, not knowing where you're going to stay or what you'll eat. Despite only having a few days until I reached Singapore, I woke in the morning, looked at my bike and asked Linnea if I could stay an extra day. The same thing happened twenty-four hours later. The road, as always, seemed a lonely and daunting prospect.

I finally left at the third attempt.

In Singapore, I was looking forward to seeing and staying with two old university friends, Teddy and Jenny. My sister and her husband were flying out to see me a couple of days later. I had spent the previous forty-eight hours excitedly counting down the distance. I tucked myself in against the barrier as I cycled over the bridge from Malaysia to Singapore before plunging downwards into a tunnel for the security checks and passport control. I filled out the requisite forms, bounced over a few frustratingly effective speed bumps, emerged from the tunnel into the sunshine, and suddenly found myself in this place I had thought so much about. I had been so focused on my arrival that I had forgotten to eat properly so immediately, and shamelessly, sought refuge at a McDonald's as a treat.

I didn't just want to get to downtown Singapore, though. I wanted to get to the tip of mainland Asia. There is a small island called Sentosa off the southern coast of Singapore. At the southern edge of Sentosa, with its theme park and highly expensive houses, there is a rope suspension bridge. A sign clearly states: 'No bikes'. Given the width and awkwardness involved in passing people on the bridge, it was an understandable rule, but I felt my crossing was warranted given my 13,000-mile journey to get there. So Dorothy and I awkwardly lumbered over the bridge and, in a most British way, apologised awkwardly as we allowed others to squeeze past. At the end of the rope bridge was a wooden sign that read:

THE SOUTHERNMOST POINT OF CONTINENTAL ASIA

I propped my bike against the rocks below it and, as is customary for a solo traveller, asked a kindly person to take a photo that represented far more to me than they probably realised. I then went to the edge of the water and looked at the sea to the south.

I had imagined an empty sandy beach, or a rocky outcrop, where I could sit and take a reflective photo looking at the sea beyond, signifying a moment of internal satisfaction. In fact, on this small wooden platform there were about ten other tourists using selfie sticks, speaking on their mobiles and orchestrating group photos. I stopped and looked out for a few minutes, listening to the conversations around me while leaning against the barrier. I then updated my online tracker and wheeled my bike back across the bridge. As I steadily made my way through the city towards my friends' apartment, I did, however, have a chance to ponder over the journey I had been on.

Back in Kuala Lumpur, I had been so close to Singapore that it was no longer an uncertain objective; it was right there, just a few hundred miles away. The internal anxiety about whether I would make it and when I would arrive had gone out the window. After all that ambiguity about what might happen, the hopes and fears about what grand solo travels actually entailed, imaginings had become experience, theory had become reality.

It did not matter how long it took or that the journey might or might not continue. If you keep cycling day after day then the miles, countries, continents, punctures and pedal strokes will increase. What mattered more was that I had achieved what I had set out to achieve.

I had little doubt that the array of experiences I had accumulated as I pedalled alone across Europe and Asia would influence my perspective on the world. I knew the range of people I had met – young and old, rich and poor, European and

Asian, Christian and Muslim – would have an impact on my thinking. Some aspects of the journey would inevitably stand out, especially the extremes – the coldest, loneliest, saddest, angriest and scariest – but I needed time to process what I had seen and done, be that from my saddle in another country, or back at home with those I loved.

Somewhere in Kazakhstan, I had chatted to my sister about potentially coordinating a place for her to meet me on the ride. I had given her a rough estimation, 6,000 miles and 150 days before, of when and where this rendezvous could be. The conclusion I came to was mid-April in Singapore. It was a bold estimation given the time, distance and variables between where I was and where I needed to be. Over the past five months, I had taken days and even weeks out here and there but that target had always been in the back of my mind: 18 April, Singapore.

The Singapore date had given me a firm timing which couldn't be tweaked: an objective. It had given me constant checkpoints, a reason to cycle a certain distance per day and a reason to get up in the morning even when the thought of doing so had seemed beyond me.

It was now 18 April. I heard a knock on the door of the apartment and my sister and brother-in-law were waiting outside with small bags, big smiles and even bigger hugs. It had been a long time.

Cycling across either Europe, Kazakhstan or China would in itself have been an accomplishment worthy of celebration. However, having a far greater goal constantly ahead of me, I didn't feel that getting carried away over these triumphs was warranted. Here in Singapore, though, with family around me, the situation was different. I had cycled through sand and snow, thunder and sunshine, and had made it from London to the southernmost tip of Asia. Quite simply, I had run out of land. So we sat on the balcony with a bottle of champagne, spoke to the rest of our family back home and celebrated.

**2.**

It is so easy now to arrive at an airport, pick a flight and arrive a few hours later in a new country. Planes depart to far-flung places of which we know very little. The option is there for us to stretch our horizons and expand our breadth of knowledge. And yet we often neglect to take these opportunities; instead we choose familiarity. In our lives of flux and ambiguity, there is comfort in consistency.

On other occasions, we consciously seek contrasts. We may return from a trip with a story for friends and a beautiful photo album or a dodgy tan line and a new passion. Equally, we may return with a renewed love for our own country and our own homes. The appreciation of what we have is put into context when contrasted with the unfamiliarity we encountered during our time away. Or as the Chinese writer and philosopher Lin Yutang said, 'No one realises how beautiful it is to travel until he comes home and rests his head on his old, familiar pillow.'

In Malaysia I had met a young Spanish couple. They were a few weeks into a year-long journey to their home in Madrid.

Around the same time, I had a friend setting off from the UK who was attempting to ride to China. Both the couple and my friend were following a similar route through Europe and Central Asia in different directions and asked me for advice. I gave them a few obvious practical suggestions but I didn't want to say too much. On these sorts of journeys, everyone learns their own routines, makes amends for their errors and goes through their own emotional evolution. This is something to think about when you are months down the line and need reminding of the journey you've been on.

You quickly learn on this type of trip that there is no point in pretending to do it like someone else or fulfilling someone else's aspirations. There will always be someone who rides faster and longer in hotter, colder, windier or higher terrain. As with climbing expeditions, you have to be honest about how you want to tackle the mountain. Going solo and unsupported, with no oxygen, lies at one end of the spectrum; at the other, a small, fully guided team inclusive of unlimited Sherpa support and oxygen tanks. There is no answer to suit everyone, and equally, there is no need to be dishonest about the option you've taken.

Leaving home in the summer of 2018 was odd. I won't forget my mum's tearful eyes when I finally said, 'The time has come. I think I'm off now', after packing and re-packing, dithering and delaying. The journey appeared to tick all the boxes I wanted from a grand solo adventure. Whether it would be enough or too much, I had no idea. But there was only one way to find out.

Tolkien was right: it is a dangerous business leaving your front door. By staying safely at home, there is no need to test your boundaries, to go somewhere or try something new. That's the reason the 'doorstep mile' is so significant; overcoming the fear of what lies beyond. It is not just about mental and physical battles when things get hard, either, though there is no hiding from the reality that cycling across countries and continents is physically and mentally demanding. It is more about making a decision that feels scary and bold; a decision that demands courage.

Part of me envied the wide-eyed ignorance and total eagerness I had in western Europe when my clothes were clean, my kit was fully functioning and my tan lines were non-existent. The other part is proud I fumbled my way through that phase with enough sense of adventure that I believed it worth continuing.

I have long admired great British travellers but I did not feel I had done anything worthy of comparison with their accomplishments. With this trip I had wanted to do something that scared me and that stretched my perceived limitations. I had wanted to gain an understanding of what solo journeys were like.

Often when you undertake a particular journey or challenge, the respect you had for those who have done it before you diminishes. You realise what is actually required and it is less than what you believed beforehand. My journey was the reverse.

Cycle tourers and solo travellers are a unique bunch. The real reason I have such complete respect for them is because they have a better idea than most of how to answer Bob Dylan's question of how it feels to be without a home. Being without a home for a short period, even when secure in the knowledge that your family is waiting where you left them, is something I won't forget. The kindness of strangers, the political contrasts, the confusion and longing, the fear and excitement, the highs and lows, the jubilation and dejection – they all mattered. Every experience I underwent was etched into my psyche, consciously or unconsciously.

It is a tough life alone on the road; to be at the mercy of other people's kindness, to find yourself totally bereft of ideas when something goes wrong and you know there's nobody else who can help. The road forces times of intense soul-searching; it can bring loneliness and sadness but, equally, periods of great joy, humbled satisfaction and, finally, celebration. That is how my life alone on the road felt to me. My life as a rolling stone.

Writing about his walk across Afghanistan, Rory Stewart said, 'I had never found a way to answer that question without sounding awkward, insincere or ridiculous.' The simple question he'd been asked was 'Why?' It's an impossibly difficult question to answer when you've been asking yourself the same thing day after day.

George Mallory famously answered the question of why he wanted to climb Everest by saying, 'Because it's there'. On another occasion, he answered it by saying,

> If you cannot understand that there is something in man which responds to the challenge of this mountain and goes out to meet it, that the struggle is the struggle of life itself upward and forever upward, then you won't see why we go.

In mountaineering expeditions, the end goal is apparently obvious: a successful summit and a safe return, even if the reality is more nuanced.

For me, confronting that question of 'Why?' was inescapable. Yet the answer, like my daily horizon, fluctuated constantly. Inevitably perhaps, it became confused as different experiences brought about different sentiments. Sometimes the answer was clear, other times less so. Sometimes, the morning sun glistening on fresh ice crystals or the alpenglow over great mountains would strike me. On other days, the satisfaction of riding a particular number of miles, fixing a recurring mechanical issue or a chance encounter with a local was enough to keep moving.

But often, when trying to understand my reason for going, I was faced by a void. I was like an artist looking at a blank canvas, waiting for inspiration. And then something would emerge again and my motivation was renewed.

Alan Watts questioned the idea of comparing life with a journey where our sole purpose was to get to the end. He said that life was a musical thing and we were supposed to sing or dance while the music was being played rather than aim at a particular spot in a room. Maybe that was the point of my journey and my answer to the question of 'Why?' In Watts's words, 'The whole point of the dancing is the dance.'

# ACKNOWLEDGEMENTS

The story of this book began before I left home and ended after I returned. I cannot list everyone who assisted me during that time. Some of you have been mentioned here, the vast majority have not. I apologise for that but each of you were in my thoughts as I wrote this book.

In many ways, this book is for the people who gave me food, shelter and hope during the course of my journey. Without motivation or reward, there were those who took me in and showed me love and hospitality in environments where there appeared to be very little. You are too many to mention and most of you will never read this but my appreciation is heart-felt and genuine.

It is also for the people who showed me love from afar and those who instinctively knew when I needed their support. Your belief gave me the courage to continue when logic advised against it and brought necessary balance, amusement and lightness.

There are, of course, certain people who do warrant specific mention for making this book possible.

Roger, your wise words and advice assisted from beginning to end and you always believed in what I was trying to achieve with this book.

Clare, you gave me encouragement and showed faith in my writing when others didn't.

Jen, your astuteness and honesty during the editing process was, once again, immense.

Ian, your sharp eye and knowledge helped enormously to refine the text to what it is now.

Olive and Hattie, for your beautiful artistic talents once again.

Kiri, for your unwavering love, guidance and inspiration throughout.

My family, for putting up with me longer than anyone else and for always believing in my unrelaxing pursuits.

# ABOUT THE AUTHOR

Geordie Stewart is a British author, explorer, endurance athlete and former army officer.

Aged twenty-two, he became the youngest Briton to climb the Seven Summits – the highest mountain on each of the seven continents – when he summited Everest on his second attempt. In 2018, he wrote his first book, *In Search of Sisu*.

After a five-year career in an army reconnaissance regiment, Geordie departed the UK to begin a 22,500-mile, fourteen-month solo cycle around the world.

He currently spends his time writing, undertaking adventures and encouraging others to explore the natural world.

Printed in Poland
by Amazon Fulfillment
Poland Sp. z o.o., Wrocław

64123822R00146